52 Ways to Ignite Your Congregation . . . GENEROUS GIVING

William C. Green

Foreword by Shawnthea Monroe

THE PILGRIM PRESS
CLEVELAND

DEDICATION

to Jonathan

SUSTAINABLE FORESTRY INITIATIVE
Label applies to the text stock

Certified Fiber Sourcing
www.sfiprogram.org

The Pilgrim Press, 700 Prospect Avenue, Cleveland, OH 44115
thepilgrimpress.com

© 2010 by William C. Green

Scripture quotations, unless otherwise noted, are from the New Revised Standard Version of the Bible, © 1989 by the Division of Christian Education of the National Council of Churches of Christ in the United States of America, and are used by permission.

Printed in the United States of America on acid-free paper

13   12   11   10   5   4   3   2   1

Library of Congress Cataloging-in-Publication Data

Green, William C.
    52 ways to ignite your congregation—generous giving / William C. Green.
        p. cm.
    Includes bibliographical references.
    ISBN 978-0-8298-1852-9 (alk. paper)
    1. Christian giving.   2. Generosity—Religious aspects—Christianity.   I. Title.   II. Title: Fifty-two ways to ignite your congregation—generous giving.
BV772.G74 2010
248'.6071—dc22   2009037074

CONTENTS

FOREWORD

In 1997, I found myself on a red-eye flight to Las Vegas, Nevada. Sin City holds no allure for me, but I had a job to do. Actually, I had two jobs to do. First, I had to officiate at the wedding of a good friend who had decided to tie the knot in the Crystal Chapel at Bally's Casino. Second, I had to bet the money given to me by my church's Stewardship Committee. The chairman's words rang in my ears: "If you get really lucky, we can cancel this year's campaign!"

Of all the tasks involved in ministry, raising money is arguably the most onerous. Most clergy would prefer to skip the "sermon on the amount" and leave the all-too-earthly work of the annual stewardship campaign to "willing" lay people or professional fund-raisers. Like most ministers, I have little training in the area of finance and, when confronted with complex accounting spreadsheets or budget shortfalls, I am sorely tempted to retreat to my office and hide. No other subject makes me feel more incompetent or conflicted. After all, raising money for the work of the church seems nothing short of self-serving and it has the potential to offend many people.

Like most ministers, I serve a congregation that is diverse, especially in terms of financial resources and personal attitudes about money. This makes the annual stewardship campaign akin to creeping through a minefield: no matter what the approach, someone is likely to be upset. There are people in the church who prefer a straightforward approach: tell me how much you want and what it is for. Others are more comfortable with the soft sell, using the metaphor of "time, talent, and treasure." Still others prefer no approach at all, viewing the act of soliciting pledges as a sign of unfaithfulness. Almost no one wants to hear that "four-letter" word "tithe." No wonder clergy and lay people view stewardship an unpleasant but necessary part of ministry.

So what do ministers do? We line our bookshelves with self-help guides and how-to books on successful fund-raising that read like they were written by Martha Stewart. We attend seminars and workshops on the seven habits of highly effective stewardship. We produce glossy brochures, tricolored pie charts, and thermometers in the shape of steeples—all designed to chart our progress towards solvency. Yet in the end, even if we succeed beyond our wildest dreams, like Sisyphus, we'll have to start the whole process over again next year. No wonder my Stewardship Committee was willing to play the slots in Vegas: any chance to cancel the annual campaign is worth taking.

That's the wonderful thing about Bill Green: he knows exactly where we live and how we feel. He's been there, done that, and has the t-shirt. Bill knows firsthand the anxiety and fear ministers have about money and fund-raising. But rather than creating another how-to book, he brings a wealth of theological and biblical knowledge as well as practical experience to bear on the subject of stewardship. The result is *Generous Giving* and the book is good, good news.

Bill Green's approach, while undeniably practical, is not another money raising technique: he's not out to build a better mousetrap. Instead, he changes the whole nature of the conversation by reframing the issue of stewardship using the language of generosity.

The problem is that much of the fund-raising in the church is framed in the imperative: what *must* be done. Even when we dress it up with the language of faith, the imperative tone shines through. Because God has given so much to us, we *must* give to God. Of course the quickest way to raise resistance to any issue or idea in the mainline church is to tell people what they *must* do. Imperative stewardship isn't effective.

Generous Giving eschews the imperative in favor of the indicative, for Bill Green knows that generosity flows naturally from people who are in a life-giving relationship with God. This is a relationship rooted in worship, surrounded by hospitality, and alive with the Spirit. In the context of this relationship, we are called to set the stage theologically and biblically—then get out of the way. According to Green, generosity is hard-wired into the human soul.

Green divides this book into three sections, each exploring a different wellspring of Christian generosity. There is reciprocal generosity, where we discover and respond to how much we have freely received from God. There is open generosity, where we learn the blessings of giving with no strings attached. And there is doxological generosity—generosity rightly understood as the truest form of gratitude and praise to God.

Yet Green not only expands our understanding of generosity, he peppers his work with fresh and provocative insights: *The church needs to be shrewd about money. The bottom line really does matter. People will not give if they've never been asked.* This work is neither idealistic nor overly pragmatic. Green has a foot in both worlds and his approach to stewardship is holistic—holy and whole. *Generous Giving* meets us where we are, recognizing all the discomfort and dysfunction around money in the church. Green neither cajoles nor corrects—he simply offers another path altogether. *I shall show you a more excellent way . . .*

By the end of *Generous Giving* one begins to see the annual stewardship campaign as an act of hospitality, a chance to create the appropriate circumstances for people to do what they long to do: be generous. The good news is that giving to the church is really an expression of our truest nature, a form and function of our Christian faith, and a visible sign of the grace of God. By reframing stewardship, Bill Green reveals the abundant generosity that exists in every church and every heart. I feel like I've hit the jackpot.

Rev. Dr. Shawnthea Monroe
Senior Minister, Plymouth Church UCC
Shaker Heights, Ohio

INTRODUCTION

Hard-Wired for Generosity

To reap a harvest we need to plant the seeds. So with generosity. This can't suddenly take root and yield results at the same time. People don't suddenly get generous when they hear a sermon about money and are asked for their pledge. We give as we live and can't be expected to behave much differently at church.

Understood as a year-round effort, and not pigeon-holed into one committee and an annual campaign, the church can do a lot to help us live and give more freely, and as an expression not just of what we do but of who we are. However, as the Buddhist proverb has it, "When the student is ready, the teacher will come." So, year-round effort or not, we may be ready right now to look more closely at generosity and how it's "ignited," whatever the season of the year and the immediate pressure of another campaign.

Nothing defines God better than generosity. From beginning to end, the Bible makes this clear. First, God creates—"gives"— the heavens and the earth and everything therein, including us, and including love and justice greater than subsequent error and tragedy. And at the end, an enthusiastic "Amen" ("So be it"). For Christians, all this comes into sharpest focus in Jesus. Through his life, death, and resurrection we see most clearly the likeness in which we are created and the future we can live out even right now, however incompletely.

As many evolutionary biologists argue, we are not simply a blank slate defined by selfishness and social software. We are hard-wired for cooperation and generosity; without this we could not have evolved and cannot survive.[1] As the Bible sees it, we are hard-wired for God. "As a deer longs for flowing streams, so my soul longs for you, O God" (Psa. 42:1). As St. Augustine put it, "Our hearts are restless until they rest in you." Or, as seventeenth-century French physicist and philosopher Blaise Pascal said, "There's a God-shaped vacuum in our hearts"—an aching emptiness apparent when we look for success and fulfillment apart from God, apart from the generosity that is God.

It's easy to think of giving and generosity as something we do instead of something we are, or as something we need when it's something we already have. Our job is to be who we are, consider more closely what's within us or otherwise at hand— and draw on that, live true to that. "I came to live life out loud," said the novelist Emile Zola.[2] Nothing shuts us up quicker and more hurtfully than the drive of personal or social "software" that makes us think, "I'm inadequate," "I don't have enough," "Watch out," "Keep that to yourself," or "Play it safe." Such thinking closets us, leaving little room to breathe.

"Salvation" comes from a Hebrew root meaning "removal of constriction" and "breathing space."[3] God doesn't give this as something we lack and must look for. God is that and, for all our flaws, in the divine likeness we are all created. "The LORD is my light and salvation" (Psa. 27:1).

We often ask God for what we already have. Blessing? Strength? Hope? Acceptance? Healing? The capacity to endure suffering? An ability to forgive? Praying better? You name it. And we've got it! It's not that we have God, for heaven's sake. But God has us and, indeed, "the whole world in his hands." God is our blessing, our strength, our hope, and our acceptance. God is the healing that exceeds our ability to control or understand, the capacity to endure suffering, the forgiveness that eludes us. And, as St. Paul puts it, God is in our groaning when we try to pray and don't get very far, "interceding for us with sighs too deep for words" (Rom. 8:23b, 26).

God is our salvation—and our light, says the psalmist. Time and again, we hear Scripture calling God the light that shines in the darkness, enabling us to see what is already there, already here, right now, however grim the shadows. The Society of Friends (Quakers) calls this the "Inner Light." They would agree it's the outer light as well, suffusing all that has been and is—including our doubts that any of this is true! Anything that is part of us, and that includes doubt, is part of God, and God is part of us. Can we believe that God doubts and worries with us, not in ignorance of the outcome, but because that's part of any love that's real? That God knows "all shall be well" is true. But what are hope and love if they ignore the rough parts? God doesn't skip the cross, nor can we.

Prayer is about facing whatever is, paying attention to it, and waiting for what it has to say to us. If all we hear is nothing, maybe that silence is exactly what we need to hear—and be (silent). Maybe this can morph into reverence, becoming something like awe in the embrace of a powerful love that exceeds our capacity to comprehend—"far more than all we can ask or imagine" (Eph. 3:20). This ignites our innate generosity, for we give as we receive—which, as we will see, says something about God as well. And in this light, justice is the radiance of generosity and, as Archbishop Desmond Tutu saw it, the living out of victory God has already won.[4]

God is love that loves us, light that enlightens, salvation by which we are saved—"breathing space." God is generosity itself. That is the essence of all else. How can we understand this in the spirit of Scripture and Christ in ways that can help us and our congregation?

This book approaches an answer by looking at giving and receiving (reciprocal generosity), giving and difference (open generosity), and giving as praise (doxological generosity). Accordingly, it proceeds in three parts, each beginning with a story or passage from the Bible, followed by reflection. Included are fifty-two action-oriented questions or ideas that are ways to ignite generosity. Each engages you in reflection and, I hope, discussion with others. These are broken down in groups at the beginnings ("Questions for Actions") and ends ("Facing Obstacles and Moving Ahead") of the three parts and are to be considered in light of the part as a whole.

This book is intended for pastors and lay leaders, as well as anyone interested in what generosity is all about. It may be used alone, with the stewardship committee, in discussion groups, as an adult education resource, or as something the entire congregation is encouraged to read.

This is not itself a stewardship program or collection of methods, but it can energize and guide stewardship planning and make it more engaging. "Stewardship" is a church buzz-word that can seem like a cover for "money" or an unwillingness to talk straightforwardly about giving. Its actual use in the Bible is infrequent. Here "generosity" is usually used instead, except when, in context, "stewardship" is still apt. A more accurate term, "generosity" catches the truth. This book is meant to ignite greater responsiveness to God's generosity, which is ours as well.

> *When I look at your heavens, the work of your fingers,*
> *the moon and the stars that you have established;*
> *what are human beings that you are mindful of them,*
> *mortals that you care for them?*
> *Yet you have made them a little lower than God,*
> *and have crowned them with glory and honor."* (Psa. 8:3–5)

PART ONE

GIVING AND RECEIVING: RECIPROCAL GENEROSITY

KEY POINT:
Know what you have.

SCRIPTURE:
Genesis 28:10–22

QUESTIONS FOR ACTION

Ignite your congregation with these "Questions for Action." Consider these questions for chapters 1–4. Then read the biblical text and commentary that follow. What questions and ideas do they raise that address your own? Reflect on the ideas in "Facing Obstacles and Moving Ahead" discussed at the end of part 1.

1. What would you do if you had more faith? How do you understand Jesus' saying, "If you have faith the size of a mustard seed, you will say to this mountain, 'Move from here to there,' and it will move" (Matt. 17:20)? How specifically does this affect your financial giving?

2. Faith and generosity grow, as we do, in relationship with others. How could relationships in your congregation be strengthened in promoting support for the work of the church?

3. What experience have you had with promises? What do you think of the idea of God making promises? What are some of those promises? Do they find expression in your life, in your church's, and in your giving to support the work of the church?

4. We give as we have received. How do you think of "what you have received" and how does this affect your own generosity? With respect to the church, how could it make more clear what it offers the congregation and others?

5. Are you a pragmatist or an idealist in your attitude toward both the church's work and what you want to give financially to support it? In either case, what are your reasons? What kind of idealism does your church encourage that affects your behavior? Is it credible? How could it be more so? Is this idealism really realistic in your view?

6 How open do you feel you should be, or can be, in talking about hard times with others at church? How does this affect what you get from, and give to, the church? When you want to be left alone, do you feel you will be without being looked at askance?

7 Solitude and silence are important to faith. What room do you make for either at home or elsewhere? How does it help you? How does the church encourage this, or is it irrelevant in your experience and understanding of the church?

8 Think of a Bible character you know or have heard about. What intrigues you? Were you to get more involved studying the Bible, what would it take? How could your church help? If what the church offers is unappealing, what would make it appealing?

JACOB'S LADDER
Genesis 28:10-22

Jacob . . . came to a certain place and stayed there for the night, because the sun had set. Taking one of the stones of the place, he put it under his head and lay down in that place. And he dreamed that there was a ladder set up on the earth, the top of it reaching to heaven; and the angels of God were ascending and descending on it. And the LORD stood beside him and said, "I am the LORD, the God of Abraham your father and the God of Isaac; the land on which you lie I will give to you and to your offspring; and your offspring shall be like the dust of the earth, and you shall spread abroad to the west and to the east and to the north and to the south; and all the families of the earth shall be blessed in you and in your offspring. Know that I am with you and will keep you wherever you go, and will bring you back to this land; for I will not leave you until I have done what I have promised you." Then Jacob woke from his sleep and said, "Surely the LORD is in this place—and I did not know it!" And he was afraid, and said, "How awesome is this place! This is none other than the house of God, and this is the gate of heaven."

. . . Then Jacob made a vow, saying, "If God will be with me, and will keep me in this way that I go, and will give me bread to eat and clothing to wear, so that I come again to my father's house in peace, then the LORD shall be my God . . . and of all that you give me I will surely give one tenth to you."

LOOK AGAIN

Here we have a holy joke. Reverence is not known for its humor, but sometimes that's the best way to get it. In one of the great comedy routines of all time, Lou Costello wants to know the names of the players on Bud Abbott's baseball team. Abbott says there are strange names in baseball like "Dizzy Dean" and then tells Costello the names of his players. Costello can't get it because these names are either not names or are themselves questions. "I dunno" is on third base. "What?" is on second. And, of course, "Who?" is on first.

"That's what I'm trying to find out. Who's on first?" asks Costello. "Absolutely," answers Abbott. "Who?" says Costello. "Yes," says Abbott. "Look," shouts Costello in exasperation, "at the end of the week, when you pay the first baseman, who gets the money?" "Every dollar of it, and why not? The man's entitled to it; he earned it," answers Abbott.[1]

Costello will never get the answer to his question because the question is itself the answer. The inability of one who asks to receive the answer is a stubborn insistence on looking for it somewhere else. We already have what we are looking for.

Jacob's vow to give is actually a request to receive what had already been given. He'd had a marvelous dream in which it became clear that God was with him and would protect him wherever he went. Jacob was also promised a rewarding future. Then God promises to keep these promises.

Is what this dream says just Jacob's imagination? Albert Einstein considered imagination more important than knowledge and called it the preview of life's coming attractions. Mark Twain claimed that we can't depend on our eyes when our imagination is out of focus. Sometimes we need to shut our eyes to see.

As though asking "Who's on first?" Jacob looks for answers to his concerns by insisting on fulfillment of a promise that had stared him, if not in his face, in his soul. "If," "if," and "if" God will do what by his presence and promise God has already done, on this condition Jacob says "the LORD shall be my God . . . and of all that you give me I will surely give one tenth to you." But then no doubt, as with us, this will turn into another quandary. How much exactly is a tenth? And so on. Never mind that of all he had been given and promised, Jacob would keep a vast majority of it for himself! Fair deal? Perhaps the real question is not what a tithe means and how much to give, but what 90 percent means and how much to keep.

We may miss much of what we have because it's a promise and not always something we would ordinarily expect. It's like being told we're a good teacher when we hadn't thought we'd be up to the job. Or like finding relief at home that had been out of the question. "I never thought he, or she, could be like that." Or like experiencing a breakthrough at church when the usual controversy was resolved.

God's promises can be hard to believe. They can come across as so unlikely to be fulfilled that they're not taken seriously. But maybe that has a much to do with our understanding of these promises as the truthfulness of the promises themselves.

Perhaps our notions of success, victory, blessing, and mutual understanding are as simple as the examples above, which, while true enough, can suggest that promises are real only if they come on our terms.

Think of promises we make to one another. Because they seem more immediate and understandable, that's often where our hope and trust are placed. But on what grounds do we consider these promises more reliable than God's? Our promises don't always come in dreams or visions as convincing as Jacob's—not that this was enough for him. But anything we believe, or want to, is "mediated," something that comes to us through an intervening source. What is that source for us? Perhaps it's our own faith, or our idealism, intelligence, conscience, or experience with others and ourselves. Not bad. But enough?

We need to rely on something besides our own disposition and some high-end version of ourselves. Consider your past and present relationships. Hasn't the need for such reliance proven true? Yale chaplain Bill Coffin once said, "Some people say the church is a crutch. So who doesn't need a crutch?"

Maybe we've been so badly hurt and disillusioned by broken promises that we're on guard lest we lean on another broken crutch. Maybe a large part of the problem is that our reliance has been misplaced. Maybe, as Waylon Jennings sang of love, "We've looked for trust in all the wrong places; looked for trust in too many faces"—and so overrelied, overexpected, sought more than can be found, from son or daughter, spouse, partner, friend, job—or ourselves. Maybe we've behaved poorly.

Jacob had stolen the blessing due his brother, Esau. He had run away from the consequences. God blessed him anyway, but his own earlier conduct and ensuing guilt compromised his ability to accept this. No wonder his giving was conditional: a deal, something contractual, a trade-off. What else could it be if Jacob doubted his worthiness as anyone who should receive and could trust God's promise of blessing in the first place?

If he'd known stories subsequent to his own that run throughout the Bible, he might have felt differently. He would have seen how often God draws straight with crooked lines or, as another saying has it, rides a lame horse. Think of Rahab, Samson, David, and, in the New Testament, Paul and Barnabas, if not also the earliest disciples who squabbled among themselves and gave in more than once to fear, jealousy, and doubt.

Jacob had what he needed but didn't know it. And his subsequent generosity was calculated and defensive, as with all the gifts he lavished on Esau when next the brothers met. Jacob tried to buy off Esau, scared of hostility beyond what Esau himself felt. Jacob's giving was like a donation given for positive recognition and favor in the sight of the recipient. This kind of generosity can come as much from a desire to alleviate conflict, internal or external, as from eagerness truly to help anyone.

So what? Isn't it what we do, not how we feel, that makes the difference? Besides, as the old saying put it, "God loveth a cheerful giver, but also accepteth from a grouch"—or from anyone else, whatever his or her personality traits. Besides, many are the cheerful givers whose demeanor may not show it, and whose unnoticed characteristics are actually kindness and humility.

Reciprocal giving looks at the prospect of satisfaction as a condition of generosity. Giving is pragmatic, functional, and a matter of what can be seen and believed. "If you do this for me, I'll do that for you." A more intimate version amounts to, "If you love me, I'll love you," when the very words "I love you" mean "Do you love me?" Responsiveness is the sentinel of giving.

The point of this book is to look more closely at the various ways generosity happens and how it's "ignited." Giving is multifaceted, as are we. Reciprocal generosity names one facet along with others considered in parts 2 and 3. It can be calculative and risk-averse. How much should we give in return for what we've actually received or expect to get?

But this attitude, while pragmatic, can be faith-based and promise-oriented. It wants to engage and affirm what we already have individually and, as a church, not to stop there, but to build on it. It often meets people where many are. Where would the church be without this disposition in its planning of budgets and solicitation of support? As with any charitable or philanthropic giving, more than one incentive affects generosity.

We are much like Jacob. Our motives are mixed in wanting to do what's good. To wait for our motives to become more pure would be a good excuse to do nothing. Besides, what is "pure"? Is there actually selfless idealism or selfless giving? What would that mean? Is the only alternative selfishness?

Generosity is holistic: holy and whole. The "bottom line" is that God is the Power, the Life-Force, of the universe in whose vitality we "live and move and have our being" (Acts 17:28). Heart, soul, mind, and strength we are givers, created as expressions, images, of the generosity that is God. We "short circuit" this and often live with the crossed wires of anxious self-absorption, at odds with ourselves and untrue to God. But we have the gifts of the Bible, the church, and one another by which we are forgiven and restored to ourselves and to God. As Joe Cocker sang, this is the love that "lifts us up where we belong" and overcomes the ways we "hang on to 'used to be.'"

This is the thrust of the Bible and our tradition. But there is no one way to understand what this means, anymore than there's only one way to understand ourselves. We are complex people given to many moods and feelings, disposed to virtue and deceit, good faith and bad, and all this at once—just like most characters in the Bible. So of course there is no one way to understand and promote generosity.

This is often overlooked in efforts to inspire stronger giving. Our stewardship planning (or "generosity planning") proceeds in a one-size-fits-all fashion, or to switch metaphors, as though the same stroke works for different folks. And we're all on the lookout for a stewardship book that will finally give us the answer—*the* best way to raise money. Confusing what is urgent with what is important, we're suspicious of anything that requires much reflection, even (or especially?) if it's connected to the Bible. "I'm practical," we say, "and so are others in my church." So is God, it turns out, although it can take a while to get it, as with Jacob—and Costello, if he ever did come to understand "Who's" on first.

In the Bible nothing is spiritual without also being material. This makes generosity more than a good idea. It expresses the Word become flesh and accounts for the creation of all that is (see John 1:1–4). Reciprocal giving is one of the "enfleshments" of generosity. We will examine further how and when this kind of generosity happens.

NIGHT VISION

Remember the widow with her mites, the least valuable coins available at the time? Jesus observes that this sum was everything she had to her name, while the other people gave only a small portion of their own wealth (Mark 12:41–44). The widow cared more about what she already had—the presence of God—than about what she lacked. This ignited generosity that struck Jesus and made "the widow's mite" a catch phrase for the ages.

"Night vision" is learning to see what we have in a different light. It's when our vision is as limited as the widow's pocketbook. It's learning not to minimize what we can't see right away. More broadly, it's also learning not to be afraid of what lies in the shadows. It may extend to the discovery that you can feel less alone in the night itself. It's sensing that what is already within and before you could be the "mite" that matters—as when in the silence of darkness you sit on the sofa and pray, expressing whatever you're feeling to God, glad that no one can interrupt you. Glad that you don't have to listen to more advice from others. Glad that God often whispers and speaks with the gentle force of a hint. Glad that you've been given breathing space to consider more carefully whatever's on your mind, elbow room for fear and anger and grief, and sometimes thankfulness and hope as well.

Night vision is also when you look out the window and see, in sharper profile, your backyard, or the trees in front, or the street below and the pedestrian passing by. This, too, is a way of seeing more completely what's right before us that we may not have thought twice about. St. Paul captures this sense when he says, "Now we see through a glass darkly" (1 Cor. 13:12 KJV). But we still see!

"Darkly" does not mean our vision is so impaired that we can perceive nothing of consequence. It just means it's often hard to see what counts. True to our circumstances and limitation, sometimes our best vision is night vision, something that can enlighten our days as well and lead to decision and changes long overdue.

Consider Jacob's experience from a different angle, in terms of its setting. When and where did this happen? When "the sun had set." When it was dark. Jacob was anxious and tired. With nothing but a stone for a pillow, estranged from the brother he had betrayed, amid the coldness of a desert late at night, at a vulnerable moment when Jacob felt literally God-forsaken, God becomes real for Jacob as never before! Overcome by awe, Jacob's declares, "Surely the LORD is in this place—and I did not know it!" In the original Hebrew that verse literally reads, "and I, I did not know." The sense is, "and me, I didn't know," meaning "and I wasn't full of myself" or "I wasn't so busy paying attention to my own feelings that I missed it!"[2]

Can we, like Jacob, let our "stones" and our "deserts" become "the gate of heaven," places where we are given the assurance of God's presence? Places where God can become real for us as never before? Remember our forebear Jacob.

We receive a lot of blessing in scary circumstances. Even though we may see this blessing only incompletely, as "through a glass darkly," we can still see it, or learn to guess it's there. Night vision is a capacity developed as we share difficult times with one another, learn from the stories of the Bible, and grow more comfortable with prayer whatever our mood, and when we focus more intently on worship. We can get a more convincing sense of all we have when this had seemed as paltry as the widow's mites, financially, emotionally, and spiritually.

Generosity is self-expression. It's actually self-centered! Self-centered is not the same as selfish. It means coming from who we are. We are not by nature selfish and stingy. We become selfish when our inherent strength is obscured by fear and we hold tightly to anything (or anybody) who offers protection. We become this way when we can't "see in the dark."

One of the dangers of "night vision" is that it lends itself to upbeat preaching. Whatever is downbeat is diminished or treated as a blessing in disguise. This is almost as irritating as someone coming to your bedside in the hospital and telling you that "God never gives us more than we can bear." Too much faith is the equivalent of saying that lemonade is made from lemons. That's not all bad—but it usually involves a refusal to acknowledge the lemon. This is denial—denial of ourselves, denial of others, denial of our experiences, denial of the fact that nights are still nights. It's when we own and accept real feeling, whether of fear, doubt, sadness, humiliation, or joy, that we can find confidence, embrace life, and move forward. We can't just do this on our own. Recovery and other support groups can help, but many of us need a stronger sense of a "higher power." God calls us into the church where we can name and claim this power.

I remember a woman who had attended a beautiful Christmas Eve service. The message was "Why are we still afraid? Why are we discouraged? Why do we still doubt and struggle? Amid all our fears, Jesus is born. He comes in the middle of the darkest night. Let's sing and celebrate!" In other words, your lemons have become lemonade!

The woman had come to church depressed. She left more depressed. Jesus shows that God suffers with us. This doesn't mean anything if whatever's hard is a pretext for optimism. Positive preaching and upbeat counseling are part of any sharing of the good news of the church. But so, too, are humility and silence. So, too, is a sense of personal presence alongside us, and a quieter message in which we can feel that God knows the kinds of things we're feeling. Generosity, like confidence, is not ignited when people don't feel listened to and understood. Good pastors and counselors know this. Do the stewardship chair and others promoting giving know it as well?

A while ago a high school teacher invited those in his class to make a YouTube video called, "Is Anybody Listening?" The students movingly told their stories about the hardship their parents and families were enduring during tough economic times. Their parents were in tears as they watched their own sons and daughters on the video, not having realized how upset their children were. Many watching the rebroadcast on the CNN news were no less moved.

President Barack Obama saw the video. Within an hour, during another speech, he addressed the class and spoke of many of the students by name. He told them he was listening and understood how they were feeling. He didn't say any more than that, and he wasn't patronizing. For these students it was as though their problems had been solved. They were overjoyed, as were their parents. Everyone knew that troubling times were not going away. But they felt listened to and understood, by none other than President Obama! And that made all the difference in the world. To write this off as good public relations misses the point. Both sides knew that listening was important.

Not much generosity is ignited when it generally comes across with a smiley face. That's a way "stewardship" misses people and locks them into what they've always given before. Those promoting support can instead make clear that they know about "stones" as hard as Jacob's, and about "deserts" like Jacob faced, when the night's cold and not just full of twinkling stars.

Whether our circumstances and outlook are bleak or bright, it's often hard to be honest at church. Niceness can be oppressive. Doubt or other negativity is a threat. Controversy is finessed if possible. Expressing how you really feel is okay as long as it isn't disturbing. And don't dwell on your doubts too much, especially if they're about the church or its budget and not, more safely, God. That's really depressing.

If salvation means "breathing space," what kind of salvation does the church offer? Breathing space is like elbow room to relax and move about without watching your back. It's space to express your own views and feelings. It's space to be less alone. It's like oxygen that further energizes worship—and generosity.

A deoxygenating force is hype or dishonesty, however unintentional. The church is not called to be a cheerleader but a coach. The "game" being played involves competition with other compelling values and interests. A game plan is needed that acknowledges the odds while being credible and persuasive. Who wants to join and support a losing team? I'm supposed to give to you when you can't deliver? What kind of reciprocity is that? Loyalty and duty are not inviting and soon wear thin (except for Chicago Cubs fans). They can't be taught or preached except as one more thing we should practice, which is not likely to change many minds, or habits of giving.

The "winning" comes when, as one pastor puts it, people are "maximized"—when they can live and give truer to themselves. This can't happen when people feel pressed into propriety, subject to pretension, or wonder about being too self-revealing, too outspoken, or appearing on somebody's list showing what bad givers they are.

Winning comes from night vision as important in the broad light of day as in the dark; "You can see a lot if you look," as Yogi Berra put it. Generosity is ignited when we look more closely, not only at ourselves, but at those around us.

How comfortable would any of us be with "Jacob" as a friend, or with us in church? Yet he was one of the founders of our faith, after Abraham and Isaac. His story dominates the book of Genesis, the overall story of our beginning. His life was characterized by duplicity and sharp dealing. But through exactly such a very human and ambiguous figure divine promise is carried out. God blessed him yet again, changed his name to "Israel,"[3] and Israel became the father of the twelve tribes that bore his name.

God must have the ultimate capacity for night vision, seeing in us and others Jacobs with new identities pending. We may not

be characterized by duplicity and sharp dealing—although probably more so than we want to admit. But we, too, are ambiguous figures, wrestling with God—yet nonetheless bearers of divine promise. What that means may not be clear right now, and
whatever it means will vary with different personalities. But that
our own complexities and limitations can be the setting of God's
grace—"the grist of the mill" of divine blessing—is incredible.
No wonder Jacob sought repeated assurance that it was true,
and would prove true time and again in the rest of his life.

Perhaps recognizing our own Jacob-like nature, we can be
more genuinely accepting of our Jacob-like neighbors, and our
Jacob-like churches. Perhaps we can become more open and
welcoming to the more obvious Jacobs in our community or
pews who are not nice in their background or behavior and appearance. Perhaps with the help of what amounts to night vision
we can "see through a glass darkly" and recognize something
we had not been attentive to before—something, somebody,
God cares about and loves.

Church budgets are often as much like "Jacob" as those in
whom generosity has yet to reliably ignite. So what are we going
to do? Be prudent and pragmatic in our financial planning and expectations of support? Look instead for something more inspiring
and idealistic? With Jacob the idealism is God's promise, not his,
and nothing he himself can make credible. With God the practi-
cality is recognition and acceptance of Jacob's ambiguity, something we all share, and nonetheless working with what's at hand.

As financial planners and as people whose support is sought,
we stretch and relax at the same time. We watch out for hype,
and for turning divine promise into idealism we can make happen. But we're on guard against business as usual and the idea
that what works best is the best work. Too easily all of us are
driven, not by God, but by knowing that giving to church and
charities has stayed at around 2 percent of personal income for
over a century. Why now plan for more, or give more?

As the Bible shows—and our own history reveals—time and
again something far more powerful prevails than any "2 percent" suggests. As Jesus said, "faith as small as a mustard seed

can move mountains" and become something a lot bigger (Matt. 17:20). So with money when, whatever the amount, it's gladly given and affirmed.

We are inclined to give more when we consider how much we already have. Remember the widow with her mites, the least valuable coins available at the time. Remember the night vision that allows us to see much we had missed before. In so doing, we are gifted with a stronger understanding of God's presence and the strength that evokes. We are once again "lifted up where we belong"—and so is our giving. Reciprocity becomes compelling.

It's our job to consider carefully what we already have before seeking more of what we need. And it's wise to remember the wisdom that is part of our heritage: "God's power at work within us" is hardly limited by national giving averages, and "is able to accomplish abundantly far more than all we can ask or imagine" (Eph. 3:20). That's a promise made in the name of God, not just on the merits of our church and good giving practices, except as these can be understood as expressions of much higher promise.

ANGELS

Remember the spiritual "We Are Climbing Jacob's Ladder"? The point is that we're headed toward heaven as we love Jesus. Many spirituals used code language that softened the hidden meaning of the words in the presence of slaveholders. Just as "crossing over Jordan" in "Swing Low Sweet Chariot" meant crossing the Ohio River and reaching freedom, so "climbing Jacob's ladder" meant climbing toward freedom—a very this-worldly hope, not as other-worldly as the slaveholders presumed. These songs influenced attitudes and behavior that could not be openly discussed for fear of persecution or otherwise causing offense and risking harm.

In the story of Jacob, it was the angels who were climbing "Jacob's ladder." Unlike many stories of angels who are messengers of God come down to earth, here they are ascending, "climbing," from earth to heaven," before descending back again. They are constantly connecting and reconnecting earth and heaven, the natural and supernatural, the real and the ideal. Meanwhile, "the LORD stood beside Jacob," on the ground.

In this light, the angels are expressions of Jacob and ourselves, climbing rung by rung toward the future God promises, then coming back to where we are right now. All the while, God Almighty is right here with us, not stuck in heaven anymore than we are stuck on earth. God inspires belief in the heights of what will be while living in the depths of what is. There's no idealism opposing pragmatism with God. They're two sides of the same coin of divine generosity. The angels are always going up and down, receiving and giving, giving and receiving, headed with Jacob and us toward heaven and earth simultaneously, connecting both, under the watch of God.

Giving and receiving run throughout the story of Jacob as in much of the Bible, sometimes in ways easy to miss. In the story of Jacob's dream—which Jacob considered not simply mental and a dream, but God's appearance in an actual world that can be walked on, slept on, and touched (compare Gen. 35:1–9, 48:3; also 1 Kings 11:9)—Jacob first gave God his vulnerability.

This is not what we usually think of as a "gift," and nothing he wanted to do. It was simply his condition and he gave it because he couldn't deny it. He was guilty, tired, hopeless on a cold night in a desert. The best self-help manuals in the world, all the guides to self-esteem or "Ten Ways to Success," could not have helped. Jacob gave in to fatigue, found a stone, put his head on it, and fell asleep. His defenses were down and he was no longer in control of his own thoughts and feelings.

As one Christian thinker puts it, "Grace can only enter where there's a void to receive it"[4]—space not full of our own hopes, worries, and calculations about how to work things out. Dare we speak and plan from such a void, trusting it can be a blessing? This is hard to believe when it comes from the loss of a loved one, a broken relationship, or the fear of one's own pending death. Sometimes this emptiness comes over us in bad dreams. However it arises, it's something we'd rather avoid. Who wants to admit and talk about this kind of vulnerability? Who wants such vulnerability to be transparent when it's so hard to live with ourselves? What "take charge" leader could let this happen?

But this emptiness and ensuing vulnerability can also make us more receptive to something good, something different from what we knew when full of our usual thoughts. It's hard to receive a new gift when our hearts and hands are already full. It's also hard to consider vulnerability an asset. We are helped by learning to value what we've tended to avoid before: questions, debate, more open and honest discussion. With the church this means making the budget transparent to what the church is all about and how its values correlate with personal needs. This risks controversy and doubt or delay. And who likes congregational meetings that last long—or, on the other hand, meetings that finesse questions with *Robert's Rules of Order?*

The task of leadership is not to put a desire *into* people to give, but to help the desire to give come *out*. People are not spigots that can be turned on and off. Like generosity, faith itself flows from a reservoir of shared vulnerability and support, giving and receiving. Faith is always plural, never singular, and so are incentives to give. While God speaks to Jacob singly, it's a word not just about Jacob's personal future but about a communal future in which his destiny is intertwined with God's people. Just as when St. Paul says, "Do you not know that you are God's temple and that God's Spirit dwells in you?" (1 Cor. 3:16), the word for "you" here is plural, meaning others, too, most immediately the Corinthian congregation.

So how can more of us, not just some of us, figure more prominently in the planning of the church budget and the promotion of giving? How can the "me's" of leadership and the "you's" in the pew become a more inclusive "we"? This requires opportunities to consider more carefully the purpose of the church. It means taking seriously how the church means different things to different people at different places in their own life journeys. The goal is coming up with core values the congregation can own. These can be refined in ongoing discernment of the spirit of Christ guided by the pastor and other church leaders.

Greater eagerness to give can be aroused by talking clearly about the church budget and what it does, including how "administration" and "maintenance" are also ministry, serving the church's values, not just being considered overhead. They make the church and its work possible. It's not accurate to rank the church next to charities based on how much it spends on itself. The church is not another charity. It is already mission in the formation of its members through worship, music, and education in the spirit of Christ. It inspires and shapes the quality of life it seeks for the world, beginning with outreach in its own community. The church cannot advance something it doesn't itself embody.

A tall order—providing "breathing space" to consider all this? How much vulnerability is involved in this kind of discussion? Maybe it's time to default to the angels! Consider again their place in the Jacob story: how they show the intermingling of earth and heaven, the real and ideal, pragmatism and idealism, all the while with God right alongside Jacob amid his vulnerability.

We are most "vulnerable," in the less fortunate sense, when we hop, skip, and jump to the budget in late summer with an annual campaign to plan and promote. Without having planted the seeds we cannot expect a good harvest. We have not engaged questions, and then beg them later on. We can't let the budget stand on its own merits and have to make a last-minute case for it. We forget that cultivating generosity takes time.

Looking at the whole year, we can plan congregational dinners, ask for more frequent sermons on money and giving, offer some form of weekly headlines on what the church budget is doing and what difference giving makes. And let these efforts include children and young people as well. Sometimes their own relative "innocence," honesty, and directness is just what the rest of us need. Whatever the Sunday school program, generosity is not an age-specific interest.

In all efforts to ignite generosity, what's practical and what's too idealistic is a challenge made unavoidable by the central affirmation of the Christian faith: "the Word became flesh" (John 1:14). Jesus expresses God. The ideal becomes real. The ultimate becomes intimate. What had been heavenly becomes decisively earthly—flesh of our flesh, bone of our bones. Here is divine life and love on the dirt under our own feet, at home with us amid our own vulnerability, as God was with Jacob at the foot of the ladder connecting earth and heaven. We sometimes make God more "spiritual" than God does.

In secular terms, this challenges church leaders in any area of church life to be pragmatic idealists, or, if you will, idealistic pragmatists—not selling out one side for the other. That's what many think they already are. Look again. One side usually holds the upper hand. Either we tend to be governed by material, calculative outcomes, or we invoke faith and "God will provide" in spiritual ways that easily suggest that anyone in doubt is one of those depressing, negative people without enough faith. We can acknowledge both the odds against us and why we're going up against them. If the "odds" are favorable, we'd do well to be just as explicit about the more we can do.

Both the promises of God in the Bible and the reality of the budget must become more transparent than they usually are. Bible talk, like budget talk, and year-round discussion need to be as personal, specific, and colloquial as possible. This requires leaders eager to consult with one another about how this will happen.

We are climbing Jacob's ladder—pastor and laity, leaders and those in the rest of the congregation. In the original language, the "ladder" is actually some kind of stairway or ramp, so there's room for a lot of us. We are reaching toward "heaven," going after the promise of blessing, returning to "earth" with this promise, all the while goaded by God beside us.

"Whenever I am weak, then I am strong," declared St. Paul (2 Cor. 12:10), who would have known the Jacob story well. When we quit pretending to be more than we are and stop thinking we have to promote answers that leave little room for question, we feel vulnerable. We already are. But this leaves room for God to fill and so makes the church more ideal, and more real: more authentic, more honest, more inclusive, more likely to bring us out of cubbyholes individually and as a congregation. This is reciprocity at its best. It's reciprocal giving with a payoff far exceeding the gift.

We should reframe "weakness." It can be the setting of hope and promise, as in the story of Jacob. Our budget and ways of promoting giving should convey, with Paul, the spirit of "boasting in the Lord (1 Cor. 1:31)," and not just what we can do if we try harder. "We have this treasure in clay jars so that it may be made clear that this extraordinary power belongs to God and does not come from us," says the apostle (2 Cor. 4:7). Each of us, and the church itself, is marked with ink usually invisible saying, "Handle with care"—the way God handles each of us.

We need company before we can see our way ahead and know that God's beside us. Sometimes in talking about what the church can't do, at least right now, we give greater credibility to what God can do and will.

TITHING

Jacob could never get it quite right. He was lost, upset, and alone in the desert that night through no fault but his own. True, he had his mother's encouragement to pursue a better future for himself and God by getting away from his angry, first-born brother Esau, from whom Jacob had taken both birthright and his father's blessing (Gen. 25:29–34, 27:1–45).

Given what we learn in the Bible about how God can make unconditional promises to questionable characters, we may not be surprised by the assurance given Jacob in his forlorn state. But Jacob is surprised.

Love is hard to accept when you don't think you deserve it. And so with the promises of God. Who am I, God, to receive the blessing you promise? Who is Jacob? Trying to make ourselves more perfect doesn't help because that's continually overwhelming and it's hard enough to believe a compliment. "Just as I am, without one plea," the gospel hymn puts it. God loves us too much to leave us this way. But without that assurance it's hard to get anywhere. We grow from love and acceptance, not from nagging doubt about our goodness in the first place.

Jacob could barely believe God's good promises to him. Consider again his vow to give a tenth of all he had been given back to God. God has already promised what Jacob states as a condition of making and keeping that promise. The usual vow in the Bible demonstrates devotion without condition, often involving abstinence and sacrifice of some sort. There are many rules in this vein. The Psalms show that vow and fulfillment are a way of moving from anxiety to thanksgiving: "I will pay you my vows, those that my lips uttered and my mouth promised when I was in trouble."[5]

Jacob was stuck in a state of anxiety and could not yet move into thanksgiving, tentatively hopeful though he was. So his tithe was essentially a way to nail down what he hardly believed—and that amount wasn't very specific. What does a tenth "of all that you give me" mean? That sounds rather conveniently open-ended—not a very reliable pledge.

But Jacob bumbled along as best he could. His character flaws, weak faith, and foxhole promise were only more colorful than some of our own. Jacob is not a role model. He's a reality model. So often the Bible *describes* rather than *prescribes* behavior—as in many of the stories about Abraham, Isaac, Jacob, David, or the disciples in their own doubts and squabbling. If the Word is actually "flesh," how else could it be? We surely have the blessing of God's generosity in fragile "clay pots."

Do we deny a treasure because it's found in clay pots? Do we deny a standard by failing to live up to it? And is giving less significant when it masks ulterior concerns about, for example, gain and status? Maybe as a "reality model" Jacob can be a role model, after all. After all, whatever his doubts about God or himself, whatever his dubious character, whatever his incentive to give, and whatever he actually ended up giving, nonetheless he promised to give.

If Jacob's "tenth" was indefinite, his "of all that you give me" meant of *all* of his resources, including how generously he uses his time and talent. Jacob's life is about more than money. And as the rest of his story in Genesis shows, he proves worthy of acclaim as one of the founders of the faith, along with Abraham and Jacob's father, Isaac.

Sometimes giving in reference to all of our resources, including "time and talent," is a way around direct talk about "treasure." Generosity was not split up that way in Jacob's story any more than it should be in our own. Although in most of the world today money is not produce ("currency" in agricultural societies) but rather what we earn from what we "produce," it's as vital to our well-being and sense of worth as were sheep and cattle in Jacob's day. We don't eat money—but we couldn't eat without it.

It can be hard to talk about money in the church because, unlike in Jacob's day when its equivalent was public, today it has become private. We don't want to violate people's privacy. To avoid giving offense we develop a habit of ambiguity whereby giving is expected without any expectation being clear, and the budget is presented in ways no more clear.

Along with this problem, "stewardship" in many churches is what a little committee does, while the trustees or another more powerful body oversees the budget. Planned giving and special giving are specialties of the pragmatists who are known for straight talk and realistic planning. In denominational bureaucracies stewardship has been separate from "financial development," which often frowns on "stewardship" as too wimpy, "weak on the ask," and unrealistic in any reference to tithing (ironic, since tithing is not "wimpy" or weak, although ways of talking about it may be).

We may have a lot already as recipients of divine generosity, created in the image of a giving God. But we don't easily understand this or know what to do about it. As with sports or playing an instrument, we would do neither if we didn't like athletics or music. And, if we do, we need practice to perform well. Our tradition of faith involves us in God's love and enables us to appreciate ourselves more completely. It also gives us ways to measure progress as we move ahead, standards to follow. Jacob's standard for giving was a tenth of his resources, however that was figured. Throughout the Hebraic and Christian traditions this was the expected percentage. (Actually, early documents called upon as much as 25 percent to be given for the support of clergy and the church.)

This becomes legalism—or a promise unlikely to be kept— when we forget that the real bottom line is God's amazing grace, God's overwhelming generosity that, once experienced, cries out for a response. Just as the Ten Commandments are prefaced with the reminder of God's deliverance from oppression, so admonitions to tithe are wrapped in the promise of God's blessing.[6]

A tithe, a form of giving as we have received ("proportionate giving"), has the advantage of specificity. If I say I'm going to walk five miles a day because that would be good for me, when I haven't walked like this for years, this is asking for trouble. With tithing we may begin anywhere, then increase our percentage, perhaps each year. For some, tithing is inconceivable; for others, it's the least they can do; for all of us, we can pray about it. But why abandon a standard just because we can't meet it? Should we give up the Commandments because we break them?

Jacob is a reality *and* role model. In his story we see that God doesn't back off because Jacob is still wobbly despite the promise he has been given. We see that whatever his character, the quality of his faith, or his foxhole "keep me safe" promise to give, nonetheless Jacob promises to give, says a tenth, and God accepts that. Do we know for sure that Jacob will keep that promise? How easy it is to act as though a promise should be trouble-immune and risk free before making it.

When we get married we're putting ourselves on the line. Do we know for sure we will keep that vow? When we trust someone else do we know for sure that trust is warranted? If we wait until we can say "yes" for sure, where would we be? Given his self-doubt, had Jacob thought again, now wide awake, he could have reconsidered his vow. Like Abraham and Sarah before him, on any venture worth pursuing we have to go out not knowing for sure where we'll end up (Heb. 11:8b). *God can't steer a parked car.*

How many of our church budgets "go out not knowing"? How many of our efforts to ignite generosity skip over tithing as a specific signpost on the journey? The pragmatists among us have little use for uncertainty and ambiguity. The idealists among us like venturing under the influence of a good idea. Both are expressed in the course of Jacob's story. But he never liked being in the middle of nowhere not knowing where he was going.

However, that's where he was, and he moved on under the influence of an ideal promise. Had he ignored the hard reality he faced and forced himself to walk toward the dawn, he wouldn't have had the dream that changed his life and the life of God's people. Had he ignored the dream he would have remained lost, stuck, of no use to anyone. There's nothing very ideal about a cold night in the desert with a stone for a pillow; there's nothing very real about a dream or a promise that fails to address the specific circumstances at hand.

Like Jacob, we ourselves are pragmatic, disliking ambiguity but having to accept it as a part of life; and we are dreamers, idealists, in that without aspiration, without some inspiring hope, we're lost, depressed, and depressing. An idealist at church is often a pragmatist as a parent; a pragmatist at church is often an idealist about the potential of his or her children. Both dispositions can express generosity. Both need to be expressed in budget planning and the way we promote giving.

Straight talk helps. Notice that God does not just speak vaguely to Jacob saying something like, "I promise you'll be all right if you trust me" or "aim high for what counts." God speaks of more specific blessings of land, offspring, influence, safe travel, and a promise to keep these promises. To this Jacob adds, unnecessarily but accurately, "bread to eat and clothing to wear" and being able to return to "my father's house in peace."

Many of us are afraid of putting God on the spot—or ourselves, by holding out for payoffs we associate with televangelists and the "prosperity gospel," more popular than ever. We go too far the other way. We remain too vague and general.

When I once served a congregation of farmers, there were seasons of drought. City boy that I was, and not comfortable with the idea that God can make it rain, I got around the drought by thanking God for our many blessings. Besides, the days when it didn't rain were beautiful.

Jesus said, "Ask, and it will be given you; search, and you will find; knock, and the door will be opened for you" (Matt. 7:7). He did not say, "Be realistic, and you might get what you're requesting," or "Look around, and you might find something useful," or "Tap on the door, and someone might answer."

Jesus was bold, and urges us to be bold, because God is bold. As with Jacob, so with us. Who are we to doubt what God can do? If it doesn't mean rain it means something just as life-giving—power that ignites our own God-given strength and that can see us through the worst circumstances.[7]

This kind of boldness can be expressed in our church budgets and our promotion of giving. Tithing is our standard. The budget can be explained to answer what many don't know about or understand.

As one example, why does the local congregation give to the denomination? Simply because of services provided—or that should be provided? The sacrament of baptism means that we are incorporated into the universal church, the body of Christ, and through the denomination part of that body. Must that remain incomprehensible theology?

Reluctance to talk about tithing itself comes from several sources: the pastor's own desire for privacy, and sometimes resentment about being paid so little; the amount of the budget (often two-thirds) that goes for the pastor, making anything the pastor says about giving seem self-serving; theological resistance and fear of legalism; awareness of a likely negative reaction from the congregation especially from good givers.

The preparation of pastors in seminaries often fails to include emphasis on "stewardship" or giving and the theology of generosity. Perhaps it's part of a one-semester general course on church administration. And little attention is given to the different cultural and class settings of church life. These settings influence attitudes toward pastoral leadership and church planning, including how to negotiate salaries and what to expect in helping plan the church budget. Even in an increasingly "homogenized" country, different regions, class strata, and average per capita income make a difference.

Talking with other pastors and church leaders in the local church community can be helpful. Additionally, what regional denominational leadership may not be able to offer itself can be found with its help. At least talking specifically about money, giving, and budget planning can be discussed with the denominational leader directly. Ideally, the regional body that oversees pastoral placement and performance could include attention to this area of importance to local ministry. It's a shame that so much attention goes to pastoral misconduct and little to pastoral conduct—except, perhaps, as the pastor is associated with how much the local church gives for denominational support.

"Generosity" is central to any pastor's call and the church's self-understanding. Sometimes the best way to proceed is not by trying to implement answers that have worked elsewhere, but by raising questions and discussing them with others, initially with the pastoral relations committee, then the main administrative body, but then more broadly in adult education classes or informal congregational discussion. After all, the questions here are not the pastor's alone. And if the pastor does not come across from "on high" but with a desire to understand church members, progress will be made.

The questions could bear on the expectations of pastoral leadership, from the pastor's view too, now more specifically discussed and with more people than in the initial interview process; the pastor's salary and how comfortable the pastor and people are with it; what the budget requires if the church is to strengthen its program; possible plans for attracting new members. In this context, money is on the table, being openly discussed as central to church life, not just the pastor's.

As reluctance and uncertainty begin to recede, the pastor will be able to talk and preach less tentatively about giving and generosity. Instead of limiting this to a couple of sermons a year or avoiding the subject entirely, leaving it to the stewardship committee and Sunday testimonies from the usual stalwarts,[8] the pastor can become at ease "walking the talk." Pastoral openness, including doubt and question, will encourage the openness of others. If all this ends up with some members angry because "the church is always talking about money," when obviously this is what it rarely talks about, there's not much that can be done. Few who say they will leave the church if this keeps up will actually do so, and—hard to accept—those who do may simply need to do so. The church can't be held hostage by anyone and be itself, anymore than we can be ourselves if we're always looking over our back.

The fear of legalism or turning off the congregation by emphasizing tithing may be overcome by making it clear that no one is telling people what they must give. In holding up a standard that has come down to us through our tradition of faith, we're not saying we can or must meet it.

One pastor began his sermon on tithing by saying, "Don't blame me. This is God's idea. And I have a lot of trouble with it, too." The bottom line was that what we can't do, or maybe even think we shouldn't do, we can pray about doing. Legalism has little use for questions and says, in effect, "Where I am, you should be, too." It runs contrary to God, whose unconditional love and acceptance embraces us all. This, after all, is what ignites generosity in the first place. Having received such powerful love, and being made aware of it, we want to give: generosity naturally grows. Tithing is a stimulus. It's a good guidepost. It's not a hitching post.

In Jacob's story, the divine and the human, the ideal and the real, meet in the most unlikely and inhospitable place imaginable—a strong metaphor for some of the hard wildernesses we face amid our own hardships and struggle, in the church and in our own lives. The specificity of God's visionary address to Jacob left it unclear how exactly the promises to him were to work out.

Nonetheless God spoke and Jacob listened. God gave and Jacob got it—enough so as to pick himself up and move on. He'd had a vision and now lived it out. However imperfect his subsequent behavior, as when he sought to make amends with his brother, Esau (Gen. 32–33), he headed in what God made the right direction. And through generations of God's people his spirit comes down to us today, to lift us up and lead us on.

St. Paul quotes Jesus: "It is more blessed to give than to receive" (Acts 20:35b). Sometimes the most blessed gift of all is receiving—receiving as in listening more carefully to others, respecting what they often have to offer. And also listening more carefully to God, receiving more completely what God offers. As with Jacob, we give from what we've received; we don't give from "nothing" anymore than we can love from nothing. What relationship can last long when one party does not already have some sense of self to give, to share, and looks instead for the other to fill the void? On the other hand, what relationship can thrive when either party is not able to accept and appreciate what the other has to offer? We all know how good it is to give and receive, to speak and be listened to, to accept and be accepted, without having to angle for approval.

God gives and listens too, receiving and responding to our prayers, albeit sometimes in ways hard and challenging, not just easy and comforting—as when the psalmist speaks of God being with us in "the valley of the shadow of death" (Psa. 23:4) when we'd rather God get us out of those shadows and remove such valleys.

Reciprocal generosity is ignited by the give-and-take for which we're hard-wired. Call it a survival mechanism without which we couldn't have evolved given our deep-rooted connection with others. Call it a way of coping with violence, initially in tribes as important as prides of lions. Or call it being created in the image of God, by whose generosity we are created and restored under the influence of Jesus and the church—however incompletely.

Generosity is aroused by looking again at all we have received, especially during the "nights" of doubt when vision and faith are dim and like Jacob we learn, "Surely the LORD is in this place, and I did not know it." Generosity advances as we see how realism and idealism are the up- and downside of the same ladder resting on God's promises and the responsiveness this inspires, particularly amid vulnerability. Tithing measures our progress, not as an endpoint but as an aid given us by biblical and church tradition.

FACING OBSTACLES AND MOVING AHEAD

Ignite your congregation . . .

9 Connect! Yes, we give as we have received and not just to support a budget. But our giving also includes supporting a budget and covering church expenses. This means support depends on connecting dollars with outcome. A "narrative budget" helps.[9] This is meant to supplement the bookkeeping version and show the "bang" people get for their "buck." This presentation of the budget headlines the church's values and shows in round terms how much is spent on "pastoral services," "worship preparation," "music," "education," "community outreach," and so on. Often church administration and maintenance, telephone,

heat, and electricity are broken down as they support these different aspects of the church's ministry.

This is helpful—but not if it isn't more specifically clear in the regular version of the budget what dollars are going where. Transparency is essential. Administration and maintenance are ministry, too, and should not come across as simply "overhead." And what the pastor and each staff member is paid should not be lumped together in a general category.

10 Tithing is important. But it's not part of the recent history and culture of most mainline churches. It can easily be— or come across as—something arbitrarily invoked to raise money for the church. Most people know there are many admonitions and vows in the Bible that make no sense today. (See, as only some examples, Lev. 19:19, 26; Deut. 21:18–21, 22:5, 11.) We don't take these seriously, so why suddenly "tithing"?

Consider again chapter 4, "Tithing," remembering the broader context of tithing discussed and the difference between "guidepost" and "hitching post." How much are you giving now as a percentage of your income (don't get off track on whether net or gross; figure it as you will lest you lose the mindset at issue). How much would you like to be giving with a tithe in mind?

11 What would the church do if it had more money? What does it aim for, trusting that with hard work, and the grace of God, the money can be raised? How widely understood and owned are these aspirations? Are they mainly the pastor's, or the administrative body's—or the congregation's? Consider ways to provide and promote regular congregational discussion, perhaps in small groups, in the context of good refreshment or a good meal.

12 Many churches have lay testimonies about church and faith in the regular course of the year. Have you considered this for your church? Does generosity and giving come up only during the annual stewardship campaign? And can any of these testimonies reflect doubt and struggle as part of whatever good news is shared? Help in advance, perhaps from the pastor, can encourage more open sharing in this regard. Why do *you* think this is important?[10]

13 Have you considered a midweek service during special times of the year when attention is particularly devoted to raising money for the budget? Jesus said, "Where two or three are gathered in my name, I am there among them" (Matt. 18:20). Even if only a few show up, this is at least a reminder that money is part of God's business and our faith. The church budget is not simply the operating expense of another charitable cause (historically, the church has laid the foundation for many such causes, philanthropies, humanitarian agencies). Such a service is a chance for thought and prayer in support of the church, without which giving is like supporting a religious version of United Way, part of another campaign or "fund-raiser."

14 If Bible study is not popular in your church, speak with leaders of another church where it's "working" and people are eager to participate. Like worship, knowing the Bible is part of the foundation, and stimulus, of our faith. Hard as it may be for some to believe, we can find ourselves and many of our own stories in the pages of Scripture. For believers and novices alike, this can be an important boost, even becoming part of daily life. It's also the way many of God's promises are made to us today![11]

15 Precede the collection of the weekly offering with more than a few sentences. Emphasize how wonderfully God works in our lives and in the life of the church. Sing some form of the doxology before the offering, not just afterwards.

16 It is commonly said that we can't have more money for the church if we don't have more members. Or, why not go after the "inactives," those we know are not regular attenders or otherwise carrying their weight? The truth is that we cannot overcome whatever we take to be our weakness, in this case the church's, without maximizing our strength.

Why would an inactive member want suddenly to become active, when the ulterior motive is financial—or even when it isn't? What is there in the church that can attract such a person? Who has met and talked with them? Not all can be satisfied; all can be listened to and not covertly resented as they often are. The same with new members.

Vitality is contagious. Our call is to build on where we are with all that we have already been given!

PART TWO

GIVING AND DIFFERENCE: OPEN GENEROSITY

KEY POINT:
"Is anything too wonderful for the Lord?"
(Gen. 18:14)

SCRIPTURE:
2 Kings 5:1–19a

QUESTIONS FOR ACTION

Ignite your congregation with these "Questions for Action." Consider these questions for chapters 5–7. Then read the biblical text and commentary that follow. What questions and ideas do they raise that address your own? Reflect on the ideas in "Facing Obstacles and Moving Ahead" discussed at the end of part 2.

17 Think of times you've given or received unexpectedly. What happened? Was it good or bad? Consider how different generosity can be from what you anticipated. How different is the generosity you receive from God? So what?

18 How can giving be at once well-intended and controlling? When is it meant to influence the behavior of others? How much must others agree with you, or be likely to change, before you want to give to them?

19 Little things make a difference. When have you failed to give because you thought you should be more generous and can't give enough? When have you failed to pray because you thought you couldn't, at least not in any meaningful way? In God's hand, "a little can be a lot." Consider specific instances in which this could influence you to behave differently.

20 If the pastor knows what you give to the church, do you think this will influence how he or she treats you? Should no one but you know what you give? Why do you feel that way? You may have good reason, but how does this affect other ways you share and participate at church?

21 Have you looked at your church's budget? What does it say about the church's priorities? Do these correspond with what you consider to be the purpose of the church?

22 Money is God's business. It's central to Christian belief and behavior. What does this say about making money? Do you think talk about money belongs in church? When are you comfortable, and when are you not, when the subject comes up? How is money involved in your own experience of faith and church? Is it secondary or irrelevant? If not, why and how so?

23 The psalmist says, "Bless the LORD, O my soul, and all that is within me, bless his holy name" (Psa. 103:1). Faith is self-expression in response to God. How much do you express yourself at church? There is much we are reluctant to be open about. Perhaps we feel different from others and don't want that to show. How can this get in the way of feeling good about ourselves and praising God?

24 In your judgment, what is the biggest challenge your church faces beyond "attracting new members"? What do you imagine God wants? Are you excited about your prospects? What's exciting about your church right now? Will you reach out to others and encourage them to share the joy you know and expect? Good feeling can be contagious.

THE HEALING OF NAAMAN

2 Kings 5:1-19a

Naaman, commander of the army of the king of Aram, was a great man and in high favor with his master, because by him God had given victory to Aram. The man, though a mighty warrior, suffered from leprosy. Now the Arameans on one of their raids had taken a young girl captive from the land of Israel, and she served Naaman's wife. She said to her mistress, "If only my lord were with the prophet who is in Samaria! He would cure him of his leprosy." So Naaman went in and told his lord just what the girl from the land of Israel had said. And the king of Aram said, "Go then, and I will send along a letter to the king of Israel."

He went, taking with him ten talents of silver, six thousand shekels of gold, and ten sets of garments. He brought the letter to the king of Israel, which read, "When this letter reaches you, know that I have sent to you my servant Naaman, that you may cure him of his leprosy." When the king of Israel read the letter, he tore his clothes and said, "Am I God, to give death or life, that this man sends word to me to cure a man of his leprosy? Just look and see how he is trying to pick a quarrel with me."

But when Elisha the man of God heard that the king of Israel had torn his clothes, he sent a message to the king, "Why have you torn your clothes? Let him come to me, that he may learn that there is a prophet in Israel." So Naaman came with his horses and chariots, and halted at the entrance of Elisha's house. Elisha sent a messenger to him, saying, "Go, wash in the Jordan seven times, and your flesh shall be restored and you shall be clean." But Naaman became angry and went away, saying, "I thought that for me he would surely come out, and stand and call on the name of the LORD his God, and would wave his hand over the spot, and cure the leprosy! Are not Abana and Pharpar, the rivers of Damascus, better than all the waters of Israel? Could I not wash in them, and be clean?" He turned and went away in a rage. But his servants approached and said to him, "Father, if the prophet had commanded you to do something difficult, would you not have done it? How much more, when all he said to you was, 'Wash, and be clean'?" So he went down and immersed himself seven times in the Jordan, according to the word of the man of God; his flesh was restored like the flesh of a young boy, and he was clean.

Then he returned to the man of God, he and all his company; he came and stood before him and said, "Now I know that there is no God in all the earth except in Israel; please accept a present from your servant." But he said, "As the LORD lives, whom I serve, I will accept nothing!" He urged him to accept, but he refused. Then Naaman said, "If not, please let two mule-loads of earth be given to your servant; for your servant will no longer offer burnt offering or sacrifice to any god except the LORD. But may the LORD pardon your servant on one count: when my master goes into the house of Rimmon to worship there, leaning on my arm, and I bow down in the house of Rimmon, when I do bow down in the house of Rimmon, may the LORD pardon your servant on this one count." He said to him, "Go in peace."

BEYOND EXPECTATION

Usually we like to know what we get from what we give. Perhaps it's a good life for our children, or at least the hope that we're making that possible. Perhaps it's the satisfaction of supporting the church, or our alma mater, or the work of the United Way, a particular relief effort, or a project for social change. And usually we like to receive something we value.

But what about giving when we don't know what we'll get? And what about receiving something that makes us indignant? It's only natural to want to give and receive on terms we understand and find satisfying. We'd rather not give to some worthy cause only to find out it's asking the city council to support action we don't like. And we'd rather not receive a compliment from somebody who doesn't care about us.

The story of Naaman's healing shows both giving and receiving beyond anything previously expected, in offensive circumstances. The prophet Elisha "gives" healing to Naaman, the chief military commander of the Aramaean army, the right-hand man of the king of Aram, Israel's great oppressor. Elisha doesn't know what Naaman will end up doing when he gets well. And

Naaman "receives" this blessing in terms he first found insulting. Here is "open generosity": a story about giving without knowing what we'll get, and getting something valuable in ways we had never wanted to receive it.

The giver with a problem in Naaman's story is not Elisha, but the king of Israel who received a request for help from the king of Aram in getting Naaman healed. The enemy king had heard from a captured Israelite woman, a servant of Naaman's wife, that there was someone in Israel who could do this. The king of Israel is scared because he has no idea how he can help and takes this request as a political problem and likely pretext for war. He sees only the impossibility of the situation; the captive slave girl sees its possibility, for she knows of Elisha. The prophet, learning of the king's despair, comes forward to help.

So confident is he of God's power to heal Naaman, and so aware of God's desire to do so, Elisha just does what's expected of him: he heals Naaman. He doesn't do so on the condition that Naaman move from Aramaea to Samaria. He doesn't do so on the condition that Naaman repent of worshiping Rimmon, the Aramaean god, and confess that the LORD is the true God. And the prophet doesn't heal this enemy commander knowing that Naaman is now going to quit the army back home and stop commanding the oppression of Israel. Elisha simply heals him. One suspects the real problem is now going to come from the king of Israel, no doubt relieved but aggrieved when he learns what Elisha has done by making an arch-enemy well again!

Notice the ways by which the giving and receiving of healing happens in this story. One would think "a great man" with a dread disease—one that carried with it a social stigma and was associated with death—would require a healer of stature with a dramatic cure. Instead, Naaman listened to a minor mistress of his wife—a captive slave girl—who knew of someone in Israel who could help.

When the king of Israel got the request to cure Naaman, he thought he had to do this himself. He didn't even know of the prophet in his own land who could give the healing the king couldn't. Elisha had stature in the story, but not at the time. But the prophet stepped out anyway, made himself known to the king, and got permission for Naaman to come to him. Naaman did so—and Elisha told him through a messenger to jump in the river seven times and he'd be healed.

Of course, Naaman was enraged. He had expected at least to be greeted in person. He had expected that the prophet would then call on his almighty god and, like a good televangelist, pray over the afflicted area of his body and heal it. Instead, already "unclean," he was told to wash himself, seven times no less, in a dirty river—dirty by the standard of the local rivers of Damascus.

Whatever his dislike of the Jordan, Naaman was mainly turned off by the triviality of the prophet's message. Just jump in a river and wash? Even doing this seven times was nothing next to something more credible that actually demanded something of him—like maybe a period of penitence and sacrifice.

He was about to go back home, fed up. But Naaman's servants intervened with common sense and simply brought to his attention that had he been asked to do something more difficult, he would no doubt have done it. What's lost in just doing what the prophet said?

So Naaman did, and he was healed. Overwhelmed, then, he wanted to give Elisha a big gift. The prophet refused. Then Naaman, not sure what else to do, asked to take a mound of earth back to Syria (Aram) to show he remembered the God of Israel even though he would have to resume his former responsibilities in the enemy army and help the king worship Rimmon. Elisha simply said, "Go in peace." In Hebrew, peace, *shalom*, means fullness, wholeness, having what you need to be happily yourself.[1]

In effect, this is what the Samaritan did in Jesus' parable (Luke 10:30–37). He simply told the innkeeper, "Take care of him." He asked and expected nothing of the man he had helped who had been left for dead on the roadside, ignored by the good people who had passed him by. In Jesus' day, unlike Elisha's, the Samaritans were despised by Jews as foreign heretics. In Jesus' story, too, giving and receiving, healing and help, come beyond what would have been imagined. The man so badly hurt, if he was aware at all, could hardly have expected help from someone ordinarily looked down on. The Samaritan had no idea what the man he helped was going to do once he got better. Resume anti-Samaritan ways, in keeping with the rest of his fellow Jews?

It is amazing how strange things, and sometimes the slightest, make such a big difference when anything of God is involved! Remember the widow's mites, and faith as small as a mustard seed moving mountains. Here notice a barely recognized slave girl; an enemy king who had no use for Israel and yet turned anyway to its king and God; a king of Israel threatened by a challenge he couldn't handle, at least open to a relatively unknown prophet right there at home; servants speaking common sense to a no-doubt overbearing master; a very sick man jumping in a dinky river; healing without condition—everyone involved in this story touched and moved, no doubt, and, with Naaman, healed. But as with everyone else in the story, so with Naaman, too: he's back to being who he was. Naaman returned to being an enemy commander helping an oppressing king worship a pagan God!

Everybody in this story stayed true to themselves, as did the Samaritan and the Jew in Jesus' story. God's will is expressed—what is truly good happens—through a confluence of facts and forces, people and circumstances, beyond expectation and control. God does not stage-manage the show here. God does not manipulate personalities or contrive convenient outcomes. Naaman brings to mind the "publicans" and "harlots" of Jesus' time, including the tax collector, Zacchaeus, who remained a tax collector after being welcomed by Jesus and changed by grace (Luke 19:1–10). Whatever he thereafter gave to God, he remained in a compromising job despised by the people. Neither Naaman nor Zacchaeus joined AmeriCorps or became missionaries. Neither became other than he had been.

Giving and receiving God's generosity means becoming more completely who we are, where we are, however we are. We are not transported into some new personality or set of circumstances. We do become closer to the image of God in which we are created. But this is not just our doing, and God's ways are not ours. We interfere with God's generosity—giving and receiving it—when we construe it on our own terms and conditions. Naaman had an entirely different idea of what it meant to get healed; the king of Israel had only a fearful idea of what the request for healing meant; even Elisha had no idea of what Naaman would do once he resumed his old job in hostile territory.

Whatever side we're on in life's conflicts—at church, or in the community and beyond—our own beliefs can inhibit generosity that often comes through the blessing of people and circumstances different from those we prefer and know best. Generosity that is not "open" and does not take freely into account differences among givers and receivers can be dangerous! It easily involves the projection onto others of values we cherish at the expense of what's important to them.

Elisha had no use for Syria and its god, Rimmon; Naaman came to respect and want to honor Israel's God but he still served Rimmon and the enemy king. The giving and receiving between them, the healing of God that each mediated or experienced, could have become the pretext for war had Elisha and his king started to evangelize Syria, or had the Syrian king made his request in the first place a condition for peace.

Think of how often idealism, however well intended, becomes domineering and destructive. Think of the Crusades in the Middle Ages. Were all those Crusaders evil people? In fact, many were devout believers who thought they were putting their lives on the line for Jesus and his church—as were later Catholic missionaries in South America. Think of our secular ideal of democracy, and the Wilsonian and recent neoconservative persuasion that the world must be made safe for democracy. Think of humanitarian ideals of human rights.

It's not that such idealisms are completely without merit—although it's easy today to abhor the Crusades of the Middle Ages and criticize early missionaries. The issue, then and now, is that our desires to give the best can ignore or disparage the different social and cultural circumstances in which "receivers" are enmeshed, and in which they have their own idealisms and dignity.

This is not to say that all truths are equal, all idealisms equally valid, all good giving so open-ended as to be empty-headed. It's not as though we have no good reason to advance our own views and values and give as much as we can toward that end. But among those views and values is the Christian faith. We have a God who, in Christ, shows a generosity that embraces us in all our own different and contrary ways and includes the most marginalized among us—the "outcasts" of Jesus' day. God's generosity is not given and received in harmony with our own politics and personalities. We remain like Naaman, like the kings of Syria and Israel: we remain who we are. We just do a better job of it.

Such generosity, when we become aware of it, is often beyond anything we can expect, least of all control—as when it becomes clear that someone loves and respects us beyond anything we deserve; or as when grieving the death of a loved one, a sense of something ongoing and real fills us with comfort and hope; or as for a hungry and homeless person when help is found at church.

The Crusades and recent foreign policy efforts to spread democracy may seem far from us. But the simplistic idealism that can be involved in the most well-intentioned generosity can be patronizing and demeaning of another's value. Unlike God's own giving, which we receive and are meant to share, our own generosity can come with "strings attached." If this is fine when determining a child's allowance—you get so much a week for doing various chores and showing responsibility—it's questionable as behavior at church, and in the rest of our giving.

Reciprocal giving is important to generosity. If it's truly reciprocal, it includes respect for both parties. This means at the very least *talking*! For example, our commitment to human rights can make it seem impossible to talk with anyone of a culture or religion that subordinates or degrades women. Yes, but because we live together in the same world, we've got to talk. If we could wipe out others because of their ways, attempting to do so would make deplorable situations more so. The goal in talking is not agreement, but making sure we're clear where the other is coming from, how accurate our perception of the truth is, whether we've stereotyped a whole people through the lens of fractional excess, how we, too, are complicit in injustice we deplore—and how we think we should respond, taking seriously what the other side thinks it must do.

It's hard to conceive of facing on a global scale what is hard to face within our own congregation. In the most rural, white, homogeneous congregation, as much as in multiracial, multi-cultural congregations, "differences" loom large. Which pastor has not officiated at weddings when the rehearsal became an exercise worthy of Colin Powell, and the wedding service itself full of the frostiness of "blended" families, with angry ex-spouses and alienated in-laws. Or consider many congregational meetings, when they can't be tacked onto the Sunday service and dispatched—when they involve the give-and-take of debate and disagreement.

When we can barely handle differences right where we are, we're unlikely to be comfortable with them elsewhere. The church budget often suffers when it includes mission support for people and causes with whom there's significant disagreement. Generosity is often chilled by difference. Far from being "open," it becomes closed and limited to more harmonious giving and receiving.

We can be helped by history. Our creation in the divine image is the source and inspiration of generosity in our own lives, as we learn to claim or reclaim this today under the influence of Jesus. But the traditional and predictable reference to "Jesus" is a reminder that we are influenced by the past. In how faith and generosity are understood today we are influenced by memory. We have the ever-present and ongoing guidance of God's spirit, through which Jesus is with us always (Matt. 28:20). But Jesus is always past before he's present. And so, obviously, are we.

We weren't born yesterday, and we have a long heritage, familially, culturally, and spiritually. Our faith extends back generations and begins with God's promises to Abraham. It includes stories like those of Jacob and Naaman. We can forget this spiritual heritage. Hopefully, we remember our church's history, our family history, and also the influences class and culture have had on our lives, some of our grandparents or great-grandparents having been immigrants and, beyond that, for some of us, slaves. Then, more broadly, there are the values of Western culture emphasizing reason and education, enlightenment and tolerance, music and the arts. All these factors and forces go into making us who we are today.

There are many differences and divisions through which God's generosity has worked over the years. How different life would be had divine generosity been limited to one side of our family, one part of our spiritual or cultural heritage, one expression of the church—or one part of our own lives and personalities? Historically, and internal to ourselves given our own contrary feelings, "difference" and diversity are what make life possible as much as earth, air, and water!

This is obvious. But caught up in the immediacy of the moment when everything focuses on one thing—like getting to the next appointment, or getting through another budget meeting—we want simplicity, not more contrariness or complexity. We often live as virtual amnesiacs in an age of e-mail and Twitter, incapable of remembering much beyond the last text message, or much beyond last week. We forget. Perhaps most importantly, we can forget that "Through many dangers, toils, and snares we have already come; 'tis grace hath brought us safe this far, and grace will lead us home."

What were those "dangers, toils, and snares" but encounters with conflictual challenge or demanding problems far different from what we thought we could handle, often far different from anything we thought we should have to face. How many times were the outcomes beyond anything we could have expected—and if still hard, not without hope? How many times can daily demands make this recollection beyond reach, or irrelevant?

But what can it mean to speak of generosity as self-expression of the divine image in us, something affecting our whole lives and that of many others, if our "self" is only incompletely remembered? To know how we have come to where we are, we can find a way ahead. How can we know where we're going if we don't know where we're coming from? To restore the past is, perhaps, to recover the future.

This is a great teaching of the Bible. Scripture is all about what God has done and hence will do, which is what ignites promise and hope during perilous times at hand. This culminates for Christians in the life, death, and resurrection of Jesus. "My soul is cast down within me; therefore I remember you" (Psa. 42:6a).

Hope has a history, and so does generosity. Elisha, and Jesus, gave Naaman and, as but one example, Zacchaeus, a history. Whatever the subsequent outcomes of grace and healing, they had planted what Jesus called elsewhere a small seed (a favored metaphor with Jesus; see Matt. 13:31–32) that they knew would issue forth somehow in a strong tree of grace. It was not clear how this was to be, given the circumstances of an enemy commander and a tax collector. Zacchaeus gave a lot away but kept on with his despised occupation as a tax collector; Naaman, as far as we know, never left his job either. But the point is that we cannot know the outcome of generosity. As for us, that outcome happens in ways that begin so small as not to be noticed—as with a change of heart, or a different way of approaching one's job that includes greater respect for others, a sudden willingness to listen and not talk so much. But however it comes, generosity arises from a history. The more we recall that history, the more open we, too, can become to giving and receiving greater expressions of God's love, financially and otherwise.

What are the "mustard seeds" of generosity in our own personal history, and in the life of our church? Claiming a spiritual legacy that includes the story of Naaman, how can we "claim" the example of the servant girl? Or jumping in the uninviting river? Remembering Jesus' story of the Samaritan, who have been "Samaritans" for us, showing us generosity in ways beyond expectation we may have resisted because, like the Jews of old, we have no use for Samaritans? These are matters of giving and receiving amid difference, where an outcome happens beyond anything we'd normally expect.

This is not to ignore equally important and more obvious instances of generosity, as when we or the church receive a good bequest, or some other special gift whether of "time and talent" or money. It is to remember what a difference the slightest gesture can make, as when we're grateful for what people do give and thank them for it, presenting the offering with conviction to God—instead of resenting the fact that all those people who put ten dollars in the plate could be giving a lot more. Giving grows from what we're doing, not from what we're not doing!

With the things of God, like giving and receiving, outcomes turn out beyond expectation, as little seeds turn into great trees, something we can fail to honor or recognize when they're still small, or strange—as when a tipsy farmer dumped a truckload of zucchini on one church's lawn for distribution to the hungry! Naaman no doubt had imagined something more stately and majestic from the healer-prophet, who would surely employ some kind of impressive magic worthy of Naaman's need and stature. No doubt he had not liked in the first place the nagging of a wife who told him to take the word of a servant girl, of all people, to the court of the king. And, again, ending up being told to jump in that river? But then made whole, healed, and blessed. "Go in peace."

Open generosity says "Go in peace." It has a history. In big ways, and little, we wouldn't be who we are without it. It's not there to tell us what to do but to show us where we've been. Like Scripture, the church is all about what God has done and promises to do, which is the kind of assurance that helps ignite generosity right now. Does your church have its own history recorded and accessible? Some congregations do, but even in this digital age, it's found as a faded carbon copy on the dusty top shelf in the church library

Do we believe that no one except the old members would have any interest in a fresh, updated version of this history? So much lies buried in our past, congregationally, as individually. Good times, and bad. Times when we thought we couldn't make it, and maybe the roof fell in or the church burned down, or the congregation almost split (or did) on some controversial issue.

Times when the church was vital to something important in the community, like the establishment of a teacher-assistance program in the elementary school, or the building of a community center, or an outreach project for immigrants new to the city.

Too often, what's called a "church history" is nothing but a record of the coming and going of pastors, usually starting from the church's first pastor. Sometimes their portraits appear in the church hallway, forbidding visages of the past. There's more to our church than that! Just as there's more to each of us than where and when we were born, and what our children look like. Young people and potential new members like to know what this place is that they're becoming a part of. There are imaginative ways that children's Sunday school classes, and older members too, can recreate scenes from the past.

One church staged part of an old congregational meeting. Having looked at church records and interviewed members from the time, the performers reenacted a debate about whether or not women belonged among candidates for the church's pastorate. Too quaint for current appeal? Maybe this can be done with thoughtful whimsy! And this can be followed by good discussion stimulated by one or two of the performers themselves about how the church is not alone in facing similar issues today.

God's generosity has embraced us through so many differences of fortune and circumstance, through so much that issued in strength and hope beyond anything that could have been expected at the time. This is open generosity that takes us just as we are and plants seeds of hope that grow, however circuitous the path to fruition.

Naaman's servants said he would do something difficult if that's what it took to get healed. So why not something as simple as washing in the river? Sometimes the church can get so caught up in big causes that it forgets the simple things that matter and can be done right now. After all, Jesus spoke of cups of cold water, giving the thirsty something to drink (Matt. 10:42, 26:35); he spoke of giving the hungry something to eat, caring for the sick, visiting a prisoner, giving someone clothes to wear (Matt. 10:42, 26:35–36). He did not speak of changing the irrigation, health care, or prison systems. *Yes*, this is critical too. It would be contrary to the spirit of the gospel to deny or diminish that! But sometimes big things that must be done can so overshadow the little things that can be done that little happens except political debate.

Open generosity does not judge giving by grand results. A person, Naaman, was healed. The enemy regime was not overthrown. And open generosity does not happen because of likemindedness between giver and receiver, anymore than Elisha and Naaman, or the kings of Aram and Israel, were like-minded.

There may be much in a church budget we don't like, or even about a person or family that needs help. There has been much in our own history that God doesn't like, or much in our own lives right now. Nonetheless, all of us are embraced by God's inclusive love. In that spirit, our generosity can grow with good outcomes beyond anything we can expect, and amid differences that often divide us.

GOD AND MONEY

Naaman was not told it was bad to have so much money. He was not chastised for having thought he could buy or pay for his healing. Elisha rejected the proferred payment but did not criticize Naaman for offering it. It might have been a good idea for Naaman to sell everything and give it to the poor when he got back home, but he wasn't asked to do so. He was not the rich young ruler in Jesus' story who was told he must give all his wealth to the poor to be saved (Matt. 19:16–22; Mark

10:17–22). Naaman had to do nothing to be healed, before or afterwards; just show up, do something that cost him nothing, and go home in peace.

By custom and necessity, we speak in generalities. Especially in mainline Protestant congregations we don't want to sound too individualistic and pietistic. Many of us are uncomfortable, for example, with the old gospel song, "He walks with *me*, and talks with *me*, and tells *me* I am his own." That should say not "me" but "us." After all, God loves *us, all* of us, not just me, not just you. Our call is to community, not self. God's love is holistic and inclusive. None of this "Jesus and me" talk.

Up to a point, this is true, and a corrective to popular evangelism. Nonetheless, the Bible, and Jesus, does address individuals and not only a group or community. Each of us, however similar, is different. Jesus saw in the rich young ruler a man who was defined by his wealth. Elisha saw in Naaman a man who was defined by his sickness. While both men were wealthy, they were different. Naaman's wealth was not an issue for him; it was a big issue for the young ruler.

In the church and the academy there often seems to be an implicit disapproval of "making money," at least from business activities. Even when it's made clear that it's not so much making money that's a problem, but how it's used, the implication is that only good use redeems it from being an essentially suspect enterprise. It's as though the only thing the Bible says about money is that "the love of money is a root of all kinds of evil" (1 Tim. 6:10a) or, in Jesus' words, "You cannot serve God and wealth" (Luke 16:13).

Those are true generalities. The wealthiest among us can agree; the rest of us can nod approvingly. But it's not as simple as that. It's not only that some of us need to hear this truth more than others, and it applies in greater or lesser ways to particular persons as different as Jacob, Naaman, the young ruler, the widow in her poverty, and Zacchaeus in his ill-gotten gains. With each of these people, as with each of us, different values and priorities hold sway. Overvaluing money and its pursuit is not always the main problem.

For many of us, *undervaluing* money is the problem. Even as a generality, being wary of money and money-making runs up against something else Jesus says, just a few verses before his warning about serving God and wealth. Toward the end of his parable of the shrewd manager (Luke 16:1–13), Jesus says, "Make friends for yourselves by means of dishonest wealth" or, in the King James version, "Make to yourselves friends of the mammon of unrighteousness. . . . If ye have not been faithful in the unrighteous mammon, who will commit to your trust the true riches?" (16:9a, 11).

Money can be "mammon" in the sense of self-centered covetousness that can take possession of a person in place of the service of God. But money becomes exactly this not only when it is taken too seriously, but when it is not taken seriously enough. Sooner or later, the need for it, and the role it unavoidably plays in life, acquires urgent and disproportionate influence—as anyone knows who is behind in paying bills or sees another tight church budget that can't be met.

Naaman learned that great riches can't buy the things that count—for him, healing; for us, perhaps other blessings as well, as when we trust in the success of good education and the right career moves, then find later how relationships turn hellish and a sense of direction is lost. Nonetheless, Naaman's job at home clearly shows he was a man of the world who knew about the importance of wealth and power. He served a smart, shrewd king who got what he wanted. To save his job, and probably his head as well, Naaman himself had to be shrewd when he returned home with conflicting loyalties. In his parable, Jesus urges comparable shrewdness for those following him!

Without money, and money-making, there could be no church, except, perhaps, one going bust. True, we could worship in one another's homes. But someone is still paying the light bill and buying food. But the issue is not only money, but *shrewdness*: keen awareness, sharp intelligence, a sense of the practical. When is that talked about as a Christian virtue? But what can become of the good we would do without it? What may be happening right now if there's resentment at how much the pastor is paid or how much is spent on church administration?

This may be warranted. But could it also be that the pastor's salary should be a lot higher to keep, or attract, good leadership? And how much more effective might the service of the church be with stronger administrative service? Instead of bemoaning "how much we spend on ourselves" could it not be that just as often we should be concerned about how little we spend on ourselves? That is a shrewd question given prevalent belief that we should spend more on the needs of others. Any good business person, any "money maker," naturally understands this in terms of a well-run business. We say the church is more than "good business." Right. But is it any less? If so, what does that say about how well we serve Jesus?

In its own behavior, and its preaching and teaching, the church can't function apart from the world and the marketplace. Many of our churches and denominations are supported in part by interest on bequests and backed up by endowments. Good values, not just selfishness, are often involved in the making of money in the first place—at least as much so as in the name of religion. The stunning excesses of corporate greed should not blind us to the ongoing disciplines of hard work, cooperation, and perseverance that account for much wealth. It is certainly an odd understanding of church and faith that would look askance at this, as though it's all basically a selfish pursuit of gain. And if it is, the church would be more honest not to ask for money in the first place.

What if instead, needing anyway to ask for the money of money makers, the church looked not only at the good uses to which financial gain can be put, but also at the shrewdness involved in its successful acquisition? Ironically, there's something to be learned, not only from good, ethical business people, but even from people whose profit is ill-gained! The techniques of many a successful swindle should not be a foreign language to people smart in church affairs—not to pull off another swindle, as many religious entrepreneurs attempt, for heaven's sake, but to accomplish wisely something good. Like making sure people's needs are met as effectively as possible.

A corrupt and very wealthy local union in the Northeast was disrupting a grape boycott organized by supporters of

Caesar Chavez, beating up protesters because they were block-
ing business at a package (liquor) store. The union had per-
suaded all the business owners along the avenue where the store
was located to support its efforts and the store owner. A phone
tree had been set up reaching as many of the residents in the
area as possible—and not with a prerecorded message. Personal
appointments were made by union attorneys with each member
of the city council as well as the editorial staff of the local news-
paper. Pressing its concern, the union cited correctly the insulting behavior of the protesters and the cost of the disruption of
business that threatened not only the package store owner, but
other businesses in the area.

Finally, one of the organizers of the boycott visited union
headquarters, and met with its leader (appropriately seated behind several closed doors, at the end of a long mahogany table,
along with several bodyguards!). The boycott leader and the
union official talked about the likely outcome of all the com-
motion and the ultimately bad light in which the union would
surely be viewed, given its notoriety for corruption and despite
its influence in the city establishment. A decision was reached
that the boycott would move to the town green, the union members would leave them alone, and the package store owner
could resume his business. A joint press release was issued to
that effect. The union looked better than the boycott leader, at
least in the eyes of the boycotters, who thought there should be
no compromise with corruption.

In the course of conversation that extended beyond the issue
at hand, the boycott organizer learned firsthand about the func-
tioning of this union, and why it was so well-supported by its
members. He saw all the vans parked in the backyard of its
headquarters (not in the front, where all the Cadillacs were) and
the food, household supplies, and pharmaceutical essentials
they contained. He was shown an intricate delivery plan
whereby each member in the union's area was visited every
week, with phone calls in advance so this could happen at times
convenient to members. He saw on a board in the front office
how the union's "phone tree" was set up and continually up-

dated, and how transportation was arranged to meet the needs of older widowed or homebound members.

In short, this idealistic leader of a worthy cause learned a lot from this shrewd manager of the "mammon of unrighteousness." There was no question about the crime and corruption in which this particular union was also involved. But the young man was left wondering quite simply: "How come the bad guys have all the smarts?"[2]

Unfortunately, his supporters in the good cause to which he was committed did not have the patience or inclination to get the point. The union was in a different business, of course. But many are the good causes, including the church, that could be as shrewd as the dishonest manager in Jesus' parable. Instead, words like "organizing support," "tactics," "logistics," "public relations," "political influence," and "community connections" have only an awkward place, if any at all, in the church's vocabulary and planning for new members or money. Many needs and influences are at work in the congregation that ought to be smartly engaged.

Perhaps it was unfortunate to cite dishonest managers when we have so many honest managers in the pew! But Jesus did—because he wanted to make a point so his work could go well. Elisha would have understood. Consider again his healing of Naaman—and how shrewd it was. He no doubt knew that this great military commander would not have been the least bit surprised had Elisha called down a few thunderbolts and had them come crashing down around Naaman, as heavenly light then enshrouded the commander and he was reduced to a skeleton before he was then covered with new skin! If Elisha could accomplish Namaan's miraculous healing in the way he did, there's no reason to suppose he couldn't have done so much more dramatically.

At Elisha's hands, Naaman would have been healed in any event. But healed in the way he was, Naaman, who was used to the magic and drama associated with the worship of Rimmon, was left with something unfathomable—something truly to think about—how the true God works through the simplest things, not the most dramatic; the most earthly things, not just heavenly, to bring about extraordinary results. How shrewd of the prophet to get to Naaman in ways he never had dreamed of being reached, and helped, before. Now that's truly a seed well planted, something he would never forget.

Shrewdness about money, shrewdness about ministry, shrewdness in how we can plan the church's work, raise support, and be about the church's business—this is commonly neglected in the church, devalued as suspect at best. Jesus said, "The children of this age are more shrewd in dealing with their own generation than are the children of light" (Luke 16:8b). "Children of this age" means people who know the ways of the world. These include many of us outside and within the walls of the church.

But commonly churches fail to engage directly the skills, "smarts," and hard questions of good business thinking. Instead, it often seems as though business minds are meant to be left in the parking lot before church, as though this mindset is secondary to a separate set of values and ideals, subordinate to what really counts and the church proclaims. Not all, but many who do serve on the administrative board or finance committee are often known as "bottom-liners" who threaten the church's progressive ways, especially if these ways cost too much. Church, then, becomes for many a struggle not worth enduring, and turns at best into a weekly shot of inspiration that soon wears off in the course of the real week ahead.

Money and its acquisition are priorities of church and faith. We may deplore the excesses of capitalism but these are not resolved by deploring capitalists. We're all among them. No other system has proved less corrupting, or more promising, for all the problems. But rather than argue this, we can be shrewd about what it means to live wisely and faithfully right where we are.

Jesus didn't say, "Until Rome is overthrown, you can't follow me." He accepted what it meant to live under Roman rule. Indeed it was to a Naaman-like character, a Roman centurion, that Jesus said, "Truly, I tell you, in no one in Israel have I found such faith." Then, without further ado, Jesus simply told the man, "Go; let it be done for you according to your faith," and the soldier's servant was healed (Matt. 8:5–13). It was another centurion named Cornelius who, without leaving his calling, became the first gentile convert to the faith (Acts 10:1–48). In self-defense, Paul proclaimed his Roman citizenship when up against unfair charges (Acts 22:25–29). Naaman himself, of course, did not forsake his loyalty to Aramaea. All these people lived and worked, and came to know God, in compromising circumstances. However we consider our own circumstances, we have as much to learn and accept from them as we do to question and challenge.

Generosity understood as self-expression requires not only that we make sure we know the history that constitutes us as well as possible—how God has helped us and our church through different, often difficult, times of hardship and hope. Memory can ignite generosity today as we look toward an uncertain future. But generosity also needs to be open to different circumstances, and how we experience ourselves here and now. It cannot thrive amid outmoded ways of promoting it. We're in a new market environment.

Old loyalties to the church have diminished as an incentive to give. New members often come from backgrounds different from previous generations of church members. Many are not clear about what church membership entails, or even whether they want to belong. Many are used to entirely different forms of giving to church and charities. "Tithing" is not hereby out of the question: it's part of our tradition. But not everyone knows a thing about our tradition, and even if its taught well, of all forms of giving, tithing or moving towards it needs most "shrewdly" to take into account the current culture and background of the church.

Too often the church leaves unclear what members are expected to give. We're weak on what financial people call "the ask." What turns people off is being left with only a fuzzy idea of what they should be giving, suspecting that, whatever it is, they're probably not giving enough. This can be more coercive than any telling of a need to give and support the budget, mindful of standards. We respect the personal decision people must make for themselves but don't help when we avoid the subject of money, just punt and leave it to them. This is like parents who don't want to have their children involved in religion because they want them to "make up their minds on their own." What's to make up their minds about if they don't know what they're deciding?

Not only must the budget be transparent and presented in an attractive way that shows what dollars do. But the faith and purpose of the church need to be clear. Someone going to a car dealer doesn't want to find out the dealer's actually selling snowmobiles or bicycles! After discussion among church leaders and members a brief, clear mission statement can be developed. It can then appear all over the place in different formats, from the Sunday bulletin to posters and artwork throughout the church, maybe even inspiring a church song.

One church group recently came up with such a mission statement. It was simply, "Hearing God where you live (and in other surprising places)"—with a short Web tag that might be "godwhereyoulive" or "411godwhereyoulive."[3] Does your church have a lively and updated Web site? Is it interactive—or just a place where sermons and programs are posted? Notice this is not just promotion of the church, but of what the church is about, and with what emphasis: *God!* Is God so somber and boring that it's irreverent to share enthusiasm about the work of the church?

Coming from a concise mission statement, church goals can be made clear. What is the church aiming to accomplish in the next year, the next three years, the next five years? (Anything beyond that is not helpful; many are not even sure they'll be living where they are a year from now, especially during these uncertain economic times.)

Good business knows this thinking in the way it sells and promotes its products. With the church it's often not even clear to many why the church needs support in the first place! One denomination was asked recently to produce a brochure for local congregations called "Why Does the Church Need

Support?" For many the church is like the public library, the symphony hall, or the art institute, albeit on a smaller scale. It's just there. Most people are not patrons of the arts; why should they give to the church when other landmarks of the community just exist, probably supported by the community preservation trust or historic endowments?

We take a lot for granted. Generosity is often tightfisted, not on purpose, but when people are not made aware of all the church is and does, or don't have a feel for it yet. Beyond a well-owned mission statement and both the promotion and clearer planning it can inspire, this "feel" and understanding happen best one on one. Many younger people and families are different from the rest of us, in background, belief, and expectation. And that difference needs to be taken into account before their participation and giving can become natural and open.

There is nothing complicated about doing this. Simply talk and listen, eager to learn about them, their interests, work, and what they value. Anyone at ease with relating to strangers can do this. Often these are business people who, but for that skill, could not do their jobs. Often they are old-timers who are simply glad to see a new face. Sometimes they're parents who, seeing a newcomer with children, can pick up on that naturally, also sharing what the church has to offer children. Happily, many other members come from diverse backgrounds and themselves recall when they were getting used to their new church environment. They, too, can help.

Being shrewd—being keenly aware, with a sharp sense of the practical—is nothing we associate with hospitality. But hospitality does not just happen because we're hospitable. Many church members think of their churches as "friendly" when they are anything but. Friendly to people already part of church life, maybe. But "outsiders" are left to find their own way to the coat rack and are not often engaged in conversation in the hallway. Hospitality, like anything worthwhile, including developing and promoting the church budget, takes forethought and planning. This does not make it contrived: it makes it possible![4]

Here again, remembering the significance of the seemingly insignificant in Naaman's story can be helpful. It's not the prophet alone—or the pastor—who makes the difference. It's not something dramatic meant to impress new attendees like, as one church did, having them all stand up during worship and be applauded (several never came back).

Like Naaman's cure, what counts often happens in ordinary ways—though hopefully not as offensive as what Naaman was asked to do! A dozen people in the congregation could be primed to say "Good morning, I haven't seen you here before," followed by introductions but also—something that rarely happens—an expression of pride about the church and what it has to offer. This means the other person doesn't have to talk more than they're inclined to; it doesn't put them on the spot. It leaves room for questions. It can conclude with a simple, "It would be nice to see you here again. Let me know if I can be helpful."

Perhaps in this brief encounter reference can also be made to another inviting truth about the church, "We have people from a lot of different backgrounds here. Not all of us look at things the same way, but we're open to all kinds of views." This may turn off a fundamentalist. But we are what we are. Sharing that with pride is not presumptuous. It's something we rarely overdo if we do it at all.[5]

Elisha didn't show much hospitality to Naaman. Namman was offended that he wasn't even greeted by the prophet, but by a messenger. Elisha simply got on with the work at hand. He was no doubt shrewd in how he chose to reach and heal Naaman. Perhaps he was shrewd as well with "hospitality." Perhaps he knew that the honorifics and the sweet talk this high official was accustomed to, and all the special ways in which Naaman thought the divine should be represented, were beside the point and untrue to what God is all about.

The open generosity Elisha showed this very different "newcomer" was all about the hospitality, not of Elisha, but of God. This is worth remembering as we welcome others in the spirit of our own generosity and seek to show the same in our own support of the church and fellow members. We can pave the way to a new experience of faith and church—and shrewdly so! But it's God who makes the difference. In God's name, spoken out loud or not, our own generosity toward others and the church will grow as we become more open, more genuine: more complete.

A DIFFERENT PROMISE— AND CHALLENGE

Open generosity is the heart of Elisha and what Naaman experienced. It's the heart of the gospel and the heartbeat of our tradition. It's the heart of God. "For God so loved *the world* that he gave his only Son" so that we can share life at its best, whatever the trouble along the way. (As John 3:16 puts it, "so that everyone who believes in him may not perish but may have eternal life." Notice "may have," as in right now, not just "will have," in the future.) This inclusive generosity extends to all of us, also meaning *"all* that is *within* me" (Psa. 103:1)—our own internal contradictions and contrariness—and all that is true of others. This embraces military commanders, like Naaman and Cornelius; tax collectors like Zacchaeus; "Samaritans" like the "good Samaritan" in Jesus' day, or the relatively unknown man of God, Elisha; "Aramaeans," an enemy people; union officials, city council members, successful business people, the wealthy, the poor, and the rest of us whoever we may be.

However we respond, or not, God's generosity is the creative power that shapes our lives and ultimately prevails. It suffuses all that has been, is, and will be, including much we cannot begin to understand or account for. Consider the proliferation of stars and planets—and dark matter, and black holes! Think of all beneath the sea, and then of mountain peaks at sunrise, valleys of shadow and darkness—and, finally, each one of us.

The African American gospel singer Mahalia Jackson expressed this well when, no stranger to trouble, she sang:

He's got the whole world in his hands . . .
He's got my brothers and my sisters in his hands . . .
He's got the sun and the rain in his hands,
He's got the moon and the stars in his hands,
He's got the wind and the clouds in his hands . . .
He's got the rivers and the mountains in his hands,
He's got the oceans and the seas in his hands,
He's got you and he's got me in his hands . . .
He's got everybody here in his hands,
He's got everybody there in his hands,
He's got everybody everywhere in his hands,
He's got the whole world in his hands.[6]

And "He's got the whole church in his hands"! But now consider what *that* means. C. S. Lewis told this story many years ago (hence the noninclusive language):

Imagine yourself as a living house. God comes in to rebuild that house. At first, perhaps, you can understand what He is doing. He is getting the drains right and stopping the leaks in the roof and so on: you knew that those jobs needed doing and so you are not surprised.

But presently he starts knocking the house about in a way that hurts abominably and does not seem to make sense. What on earth is He up to? The explanation is that He is building quite a different house from the one you thought of—throwing out a new wing here, putting on an extra floor there, running up towers, making courtyards.

You thought you were going to be made into a decent little cottage; but God is building a palace. He intends to come and live in it Himself.[7]

Are we looking forward to becoming a nicer version of who we already are? Or is a very different hope before us? Are we preparing to become a palace! Remember, what's at stake is God's promise, not our dreams. This need not mean a mega-church or another Crystal Cathedral—or temples like that of Rimmon's that Naaman considered the way a good place of worship ought to look and which he still served.

God's promise may not mean a big church and pews full of people. But it means a people full of God. That's again the "mustard seed" God plants that, one way or another, yields great results. That's the faith that can "move mountains." Through it all it's the receiving and giving of God's open generosity that makes this possible. And this generosity is open and inclusive, not only comprising diversity racially, ethnically, and in terms of sexual orientation and gender identity, but thereby, and as a greater challenge, comprising divisive views and values.

This cauldron of actual or potential trouble can be a kettle of learning and understanding. Like tears welling up within us, or laughter we can barely contain, God's generosity is waiting to spill out—or, better, to explode! The fireworks may not light up the town—but they will light up the church—and, sooner or later, others as well.

In church, with the gospel at hand, do we know we're sitting on a powder keg? As Annie Dillard put it, "We should all be wearing crash helmets. Ushers should issue life preservers and signal flares; they should lash us to our pews."[8] God's powerful love, often domesticated and turned into being nicer and liking each other, literally transforms lives. It makes us, beyond just nicer or better, even good! It makes us see how much we've denied or held back, good and bad, that cries out for expression, and for encouragement beyond a tolerant pat of the back.

God's life-changing love, God's generosity, gets us in touch with hope and confidence beyond anything we'd known or thought possible. It makes us want to change—to do justice to ourselves, and in the world itself, as best we can. Change not because we must, as the communion invitation puts it, but because now *we may!*

"You are the light of the world," said Jesus. "No one after lighting a lamp puts it under the bushel basket, but on the lampstand, and it gives light to all in the house. In the same way, let your light shine before others, so that they may see your good works and give glory to your Father in heaven" (Matt. 5:14a, 15–16).

In this light we can look again at the challenge churches face today. It's different from the challenge of earlier days when the church was as much a given part of life as was the temple in Naaman's day. Once the church was supported as much by taxes and the city treasury as by church pledges. Being a church member was being a good citizen and usually a requisite for civic and commercial success. Much depended on the standing of the pastor with the establishment. The church focused on the conduct of congregants, often including political behavior. Now we want a pastor with good standing in the community, but that doesn't come automatically; and since we're lucky to have congregants we'd rather not meddle with conduct lest we risk losing any of those congregants.

The financial concern endemic in the church today is a good lens through which to look at the different challenge we now face. Understanding this challenge can "prepare the way" to act on God's great promise for the church. (Isaiah 40:3, Matthew 3:3, and Matthew 11:10 instruct that we do just this: "prepare the way for the LORD, a highway for our God"—which means, not less, but more than invoking God's name, saying prayers, and asking for blessing before a meeting.)

As we see with Naaman, the change that came over him did not involve a change in residence, a career move, or otherwise fixing problems back home. His habits of giving were not corrected. He still gave in ways he always had, and to Rimmon— although with some mounds of earth from the land of the true God lying around somewhere to remind him where now his loyalty ultimately lay.

But Elisha's unconditional "Shalom . . . Go in peace"—go in wholeness and happiness; and Naaman's "loads of earth," both signify the different promise and challenge actually at stake: the promise that Naaman, now healed, could be more fulfilled and happy than ever before; while he returned to life as usual he was not the same man. He was now centered in the power of a love that cannot be contained and that promised to sustain him, and possibly to transform others, too, as he had been transformed. Perhaps this happened first simply though the niches and crevices of current circumstance. We don't know the rest of the story. But we can bet it didn't just stop there.

Naaman came to see that the healing the true God promised through the prophet was far different from any other promise he had known. The prophet knew not to "fix" him with a set of divine healing techniques: this was not God's way and would just confirm Naaman's old expectations of the way a good god was supposed to behave. Elisha's job was to introduce Naaman to a whole new experience of God—and through means so different as to stun Naaman while proving the condition of his cure.

Naaman would already have pursued the usual sources of healing in Aramaea. His first thought would not have been to stand leprously in front of his king, pleading for help. But seeing the condition of his right-hand man, the king was not about to tell Naaman to try again and find a cure in their own religion. He would have, had he thought this would work, instead of lowering himself to write to the powerless king of a defeated enemy serving, in his eyes, a pagan god.

As with Naaman, when there's a problem, sometimes "trying harder" is not the best response. Said W. C. Fields, "Try, try, try again, then quit: no use being a damned fool about it." To determine when it's time to try something else instead of persisting with different ways of doing the same thing, it's essential to understand the difference between *technical* and *adaptive* challenges.[9]

A technical challenge lends itself to cure, remedy, or redress within largely given conditions: a car breaks down and a mechanic goes to work (usually you don't seek an alternative means of transportation, like riding a bus for any longer than necessary, or buying a motorcycle). Or a child breaks her arm, and orthopedic surgery does the trick (you don't suggest amputating the arm or putting the child up for adoption). Or the body succumbs to infection, and the right antibiotic is pre-scribed (you don't just get more rest and exercise).

An adaptive challenge involves not just a problem but the circumstances, the conditions, in which the problem is embed-ded. It entails a conflict over values and purposes and their sit-uational consequences. Examples abound: poverty at home and abroad; the economy and unemployment; drug abuse; environ-mental pollution; crime. Many think these are technical prob-lems, and hence they propose technical solutions—like "three strikes and you're out," or "jail those corrupt CEOs" as though extended prison terms will resolve the crime problem or greed on Wall Street.

An adaptive challenge calls into question the conditions in which problems arise and requires that underlying issues be ad-dressed. Comparable to the challenges just listed, heart disease, for example, admits of no simple cure: it raises questions of stress and lifestyle, and requires of an individual that his or her values and priorities be changed to accord with the reality at hand (you'll die if you keep living the way you are; you'll have a healthier and happier life if you understand the conditions that must be changed, and *change*).

When stewardship—or generosity—is understood as a tech-nical challenge it looks for greater effectiveness within largely continuing conditions: the church and denomination more or less as they've always been, and so with approaches to mem-bership and mission, except for various forms of tinkering and razzle-dazzle. When stewardship is understood this way it looks for better, more efficient ways of arranging deck chairs on the Titanic—or more effective ways of mobilizing attendance at the ship's evening band concert, or, at best, finding new means of plugging the holes of the sinking vessel.

As a technical challenge, stewardship, or "igniting generos-ity," looks for weatherproof matches, "fixes," the latest cures and remedies for weak commitment—preferably mixed in with some colorful version of the thunderbolts Naaman had expected to herald healing. As an adaptive challenge, stewardship looks at the conditions in which giving in any form ("time, talent, or treasure") arises as a problem: an aging and otherwise declining membership base, a church program and mission structure that, however attractively dressed up, conflict with other values and priorities, the demographics that work against church revitalization, lack of clarity about our identity and a corresponding absence of a clear and compelling sense of mission.

When efforts to ignite generosity are understood as an adaptive challenge they explore other ways to sail than by plugging holes or tinkering with accommodations. Switch the analogy from a ship to a corporation, then to a denomination, then to the local congregation: *any system is designed for the results it is getting.*

This is as true of our own bodies as it is the body of the church! If you feel depressed for a day, you've produced trillions and trillions of new brain cells that have receptors calling out for depressed-type peptides "all cupping their little hands around their mouths like tiny megaphones shouting, 'Send us more depression.'" So, ironically, our own brain system can get designed with the result that we positively *need* more gloomy thoughts. We become addicted to gloominess![10]

We also face a different and happier possibility—an old promise understood in the light of today: that God wants to make us a "temple," a new system-design, not just "a nice little cottage." We face a challenge different from what we have faced before. In church and culture, we have undergone systemic and adaptive change given which technical responses are of little avail. Conditions of life and faith today are generating all kinds of new "brain cells," some multiplying exponentially in different kinds of gloominess—or different kinds of hope—often arbitrarily and out of circumstances no longer controllable or predictable.

People wanting to trust are more skeptical. People given to "believing" are less given to "belonging." People once drawn to established forms of giving as well as younger people now give selectively to specific causes with which they can identify and get involved. Much that was routine is now spontaneous. These are just a few of the symptoms of an underlying change in how life is experienced, across generations, during the turbulent, or at least fluid, circumstances we face.

Knowing this, we need to watch out that we're not still responding out of habit with "technical" responses. The system for the results we want to get cannot be like systems of old. It cannot be, or just be, planned, graphed, charted, or measured in the same way. Living in "fluid" times, given to spontaneous and sometimes sporadic attendance and giving, we need to think "fluidly." Many of us are thinking fluidly; for one example, we offer worship at completely different times with different formats, and sometimes in the back room of a local restaurant, or (not all will like this) in the back room of a favorite tavern!

Giving itself has not dried up. It's just gone elsewhere. All kinds of generosity are eager to find expression, albeit in new ways. Sometimes breaking up a unified budget and offering giving opportunities for different ministries of the church can ignite giving otherwise squelched when promoted for a general fund. Narrative budgets are more important than ever—budgets that tell the story of what the church does, divided into areas of specific service. Perhaps these areas could be called not, predictably, "worship," "music," "education," or "community outreach," but, say, "We hear God speaking!," "Exciting music for all ages!" "Education programs catch fire!" "Members stir up the community." (What church members do on the job or in the community are particular ministries as important as what the church budget supports, and, well-noted, enhance the appeal of the church.) Repeated appeals for support and participation, even for the same thing, are important. Advertisers know the importance of repetition. So should we!

Pledging and formal church membership are still important, but not as much as before. Engaging participants given to neither is still meeting needs and doing the work of the church. The numbers of pledges and new members is no longer the best measure of progress.

There is much more interest today in Bible study than we commonly suppose. The interest in "spirituality" prevailing outside the church can resonate in Bible study that is not just "Walking with Mark During Jesus' Last Days." An appealing emphasis could be "Finding God Right Now" (or, if the pastor prefers, "How God Finds Us Right Now"). Many churches offer yoga classes as Christian spiritual expression that isn't full of incense and Tibetan wind chimes—although why not? We should not underestimate the interest of many older people in all this. The old adage "Variety is the spice of life" applies to them, too. Diversity in church planning can be more than a technical fix focused on promoting attendance at events—rather, a longer-term adaptive response to underlying change.

Worship is the gateway to the church and what it's all about—and you can't have fire in the pews if there's ice in the pulpit! But without downplaying the vital role of the pastor—and the choir—we should remember that the light in the eyes of those up front will dim in the hearts of the pew if not backed up fast—by hospitality and a church program (no pastor alone can inspire and manage) and by planning open to difference beyond what most of us have experienced in church before.

Generosity thrives on difference. By nature, it's open. It's closed by reluctance to take on anything new. What if we lived this way on the job or at home? Consider corporations locked in ways of the past. Think of any of us when we'd rather play it safe, not do much we haven't done before, retreat to the same circle of friends, or zone out before the computer or television. Think of relationships, maybe our own, that amount to what Father Trevor Huddleston called "two people huddled together in the pale light of an insufficient answer to a question they're afraid to ask: why are we together?"[11]

We're together in the church, not to huddle together, comforted by the pale light of what's safe and familiar. We're together in the church, not because we're used to each other, or like each other (although often we do). We're together because we're good for each other. We're together not to change the world, but to show what God does for the world, beginning with us. We're meant to live out God's promise for us all, well put by the prophet Jeremiah. "'I know the plans I have for you,' says the LORD, 'plans for your welfare and not for harm, to give you a future with hope'" (Jer. 29:11). Regardless of what it holds, this is a future into which, with Naaman, we can "Go in peace." God's generosity is far greater than anything that could stand in our way. So it can be with our own.

FACING OBSTACLES AND MOVING AHEAD

Ignite your congregation . . .

25 We often hear about how we need to be more diverse and inclusive as a congregation. And we're asked to give generously to a budget, community outreach, and the church's wider mission that often include diverse programs, projects, people, or "causes." We can believe in diversity so long as it doesn't differ with what we know and like. Disagreement often arouses controversy, and support weakens accordingly. But how can any of us be committed to "diversity and inclusivity" *external* to ourselves when we have not faced that very same issue *internally* within ourselves—not just internal to our congregation, but inside each of us?

When the psalmist says "all that is within me" is meant to bless God, he did not say "within us" but "within *me*," and he did not say "some" of which is in me—probably the nice part—but "*all* that is within me," which means the hard parts, too. We're given to different drives, desires, and conduct, sinful as well as good. We have different kinds of anger and resentment, as well as

fond hopes and dreams. Not all of this is easy to acknowledge and live with, much less share. Not all of this should
be shared, at least publicly.

Making peace with our own internal diversity, and
making sure we're honestly "inclusive" in our own self-
understanding, is essential to respecting the same thing in
the church and beyond. We can't do justice to others if we
haven't done justice to ourselves!

The pastor's help, and that of discussion in an adult
education series, can help. Any good Bible selection can be
a good introduction, including the psalms and stories like
those of Abraham, Isaac, Jacob, or Paul. The Bible is not
full of people who had it all together! That's why we can
relate to them.

26 Debt plagues many of us, pastors too. Undealt with it can
inhibit generosity in almost every way. Emotionally and
financially, debt can make us withdrawn, ashamed, and
afraid. There may be good reasons for debt, not all of it
attributable to poor spending habits. Consumer credit
counseling is available. What about spiritual credit
counseling? Often the issue is not simply learning how to
live within our means, and what to do if we can't. At stake
can be problems with conflicting attitudes and pressures
involving spouses or partners, anxiety about personal
security that can be immobilizing, or self-consciousness
about personal inadequacy. These are as much matters
of faith as finance.

How open is the church to helping members deal with
debt? The pastor, or one of his or her staff, could help or
could also arrange consultation with a lay professional of
faith whose practical advice could be offered with spiritual
awareness. The pastor's respect for the problem is important
to restore hope and self-confidence.

27 Healing involves mind and spirit, not just body. Does your
church offer services of healing? Or classes on healing?
Most books of worship include liturgies of healing. Good

classes can be, not therapy sessions, but Bible-based, centering on stories like Naaman's or the good Samaritan, drawing attention to the unexpected ways God works to heal. Issues of healing often affect faith, not health alone, reflecting concerns about money and giving when personal security is threatened.

Generosity is ignited in our souls before it can find expression in our lives. It's a matter of personal wellness, "wholeness," before it can bear fruit in other ways. Any year-round stewardship effort focused on faith, and not only the budget, should take "healing" into account in its own right, apart from any talk about "giving."

28 Simple and engaging resources for use by leaders and for congregational distribution are readily available that can encourage good talk about money and the church. Three such resources are: "Are You Ready to Talk about Your Church?" "16 Ways to Say, 'I love My Church,'"and "Are You Ready to Talk about Money in Your Church?" Such resources can be used as they are by church members and can also serve as helpful introductions to training sessions to reach outsiders or energize those already active.[12]

29 Ask business people[13] to talk about their work as ministry: how they do what they do, what they're trying to accomplish, skills they think serve the church or could, and how their work connects with their own spiritual journey. Some churches have Lenten programs involving weekly lay presentations as part of short services. This is recognition that can be extended to members in different walks of life in the spirit of knowing better who we are. When people are recognized, and not just for service on boards and committees, they become more open and generous in ways we relate to the church.

30 Plan and promote an attractive congregational dinner focused on a divisive issue. Meet with people on different sides of the issue and find one among them willing to

speak briefly on the issue at hand. This is not a congregational meeting. The goal is not consensus but conversation.

Those who think this is naïve or "leading with our
chin" should ask whether the greater risk is trying to
avoid controversy when people's own faith is often at
issue, not just their lack of it. This makes conflict a con-
tinual undercurrent corroding good will and generosity.
Instead, we can work "shrewdly" on modeling and
strengthening what community is all about. We can show
how it depends not on liking or disliking, not on agree-
ing, acquiescing, or tolerating. It depends on listening, acceptance, and respect. It's an expression of "open generosity" and "giving amid difference," that puts forth our
own views and values in the spirit of engaging others.
This is how minds and hearts are most likely to change—
including sometimes our own.

31 Discuss "technical" and "adaptive" challenges as experienced personally and with problems in our community and
society at large. The church reflects culture as much as it
tries to shape or transform it. We reflect still prevailing
tendencies to apply "fix-it" solutions that neglect underlying conditions such as changes in attitudes toward giving,
a preference for spirituality over organized religion, an
affinity for spontaneity over habit, and so forth.

In such discussion, also consider matters easily
neglected: the ongoing importance of tradition; the need
for a sense of connectedness and of something worth pro-
tecting and preserving during times when many are, or
feel, uprooted and directionless. Sometimes more change
is the last thing prospective members want. At least they
want more than change.

32 Develop an adaptive church budget and giving program
that is open to change and to unexpected expressions of
financial support. Circumstances are not as fixed in church
as they used to be, anymore than they are anywhere else.
Consider ways of promoting support for the church's pro-

gram and ministries throughout the year, beyond what could have been budgeted.

Adaptive financial planning still involves budgeting. But we should watch out about locking our expectations, and people's giving, into predetermined categories. Church leaders can model the "open generosity" they would like to see by not assuming this is unrealistic and planning more hopefully and expectantly. This will ignite greater interest in what the church offers and wants to offer!

PART THREE

GIVING AS PRAISE: DOXOLOGICAL GENEROSITY

KEY POINT:

What's true is more than useful.

SCRIPTURE:

Romans 8:31b–39

QUESTIONS FOR ACTION

Ignite your congregation with these "Questions for Action." Consider these questions for chapters 8–10. Then read the biblical text and commentary that follow. What questions and ideas do they raise that address your own? Reflect on the ideas in "Facing Obstacles and Moving Ahead" discussed at the end of part 3.

33 Some time ago J. B. Phillips wrote *Your God Is Too Small*. More recently William Placher wrote *The Domestication of Transcendence*. A therapist speaks of "the infantilizing" of God. It was once common to speak of "almighty God" and the majesty, honor, and glory of God. Now there is concern that this is too "hierarchical" and, emphasizing power, models authority *over* us, instead of love *for* us and friendship or partnership *with* us. How do you feel about this? What does this say about how you understand giving, and particularly "giving to God"?

34 Is generosity altruism? What understanding of giving does your church promote? Does this correspond with what you believe?

35 How does your faith "feel" to you? How does your church address your own feelings? In your view, when people don't feel like giving, can generosity grow toward the church and beyond?

36 Is your church useful? What would happen were your church to shut down next week?

37 What do you think of the argument that the church is "too institutional," its organization and physical plant not essential to faith? What is the alternative? Why or why not is that preferable?

38 Do you feel recognized at church? Why is that important to you, and to others? How can that happen more effectively?

39 Are you a minister? Do you have a calling? Consider how those terms do or don't apply to you as a parent, a person with a job, a friend, someone active in the community, or a church member. Psychologists speak of how "reframing" who we are and what we face can be helpful. Instead of thinking of jobs and responsibility, and trouble or success, as just that, they urge us to see these as ways into a better understanding of ourselves and our prospects for moving ahead. What reframing could be helpful to you—and to your church in the ways it presents its needs?

40 How would you summarize "the good news of the gospel"? Some simply say, "Jesus saves!" or "Our sins are forgiven and we have eternal life," or "in Christ, there's hope for the world." How would you put it? What bearing does that have on giving to the church? If the church is not as clear as you think it could be in its message, in what ways could you help?

41 How has God's power changed your life? How is this shared at church? Some consider this "too personal" to get into with others. What bearing does this have on how giving and generosity are understood and expressed?

42 A Sunday school youngster once scrawled in chalk on the pavement of the church parking lot, "I hate God. I love the church." We're often reminded that we are first and foremost to love God—that's the issue. The church is secondary. What can you say in support of the child? In what ways do you, loving God, *love your church?*

PAUL PRAISES GOD
Romans 8:31b–39

If God is for us, who is against us? He who did not withhold his own Son, but gave him up for all of us, will he not with him also give us everything else? . . . Who will separate us from the love of Christ? Will hardship, or distress, or persecution, or famine, or nakedness, or peril, or sword? . . . No, in all these things we are more than conquerors through him who loved us. For I am convinced that neither death, nor life, nor angels, nor rulers, nor things present, nor things to come, nor powers, nor height, nor depth, nor anything else in all creation, will be able to separate us from the love of God in Christ Jesus our Lord.

BEYOND GRATITUDE

It's not we who aspire to God but God who aspires to us. God is like Michelangelo who, knowing the stone, sees the *Pieta*. We are not created out of nothing but crafted out of a passionate love from which nothing can separate us, and against which nothing else can finally prevail.

When, with or without specific human loves to express this, we know it, we find fulfillment that can never be self-centered. It's not our culture's "I do a lot, therefore I am." It's not Descartes' famous dictum, "I think, therefore I am." It's "I am loved, therefore I am."

Being loved openly and unconditionally we become who we are by sharing that love. "I am loved, therefore I am generous." Love is irrepressible and, as it is experienced, so is generosity.

Sometimes gifts cannot be repaid. Whether it's having a wallet returned that had been dropped in the drug store parking lot, a woman at church who, sensing something upsetting, says "I'm thinking of you" and clearly means it, or what a parent or friend made possible, it's hard to repay generosity. And sometimes we don't like feeling indebted—as when a friend unexpectedly gives us a Christmas gift and we had not given one ourselves. I was struck by the response of a stranger who had helped carry a load of big boxes to the car, making several trips back and forth on a stormy day. Nonplussed, I said, "Thank you!" He smiled and said, "Pass it on."

So with God's love. The word to us is "Pass it on!" Generosity takes off when giving itself is the payoff. This is more than the reciprocal satisfaction of something good given and received. It's more than altruism and doing something charitable for a worthy cause. These are good, of course. But they can miss the point. At heart, we give because God is a giver and that's how we're created, how we are. We are meant to be givers of God's own act of giving, as we know this in Jesus Christ.

Whether or not such words are spoken or thought, this happens in ways simple and profound. It can happen with strangers and friends alike, even when it's merely picking up the bulletins in the pews after Sunday worship, telling someone how nice he or she looks, or commenting on the good job somebody did. This is actually giving as an act of praise. It is its own reward, reflecting or expressing something we care about.

Praising gives honor to something we cherish and prize (the root of "praise"), whether it's family, friends, the church, or others. Christian giving is as much *praise*-giving as "thanksgiving." We praise God and so prize the love we know that, often unaware of what we're doing, we instinctively want to pass it on. It's like a compliment that makes you feel so good that your mood changes and suddenly you're smiling, now as drawn to others as they are to you.

As a biblical scholar points out, in Hebrew there is no word for thanks. In other languages as well, "to thank" is a secondary formation lacking its own root. It becomes an independent verb by the later development of a more complex verb—as in both German and English, where "to thank" is a variant of the verb "to think" (recall *danken* and *denken*). The Hebrew sense of "thanks" is actually closest to the way it's expressed in Russian by a word that means "to give honor." In Scripture the expression of thanks to God is included in honor: it is a way of praising.[1] Speaking Aramaic but writing in Greek, the New Testament writers maintain the Hebrew emphasis and so do we when we sing hymns like "For the Beauty of the Earth," with the refrain, "God of all, to you we raise this our hymn of grateful praise." Grateful is an adjective, praise the noun and main point.

When thanking is seen as important but secondary—part of praising, but not the heart—this is a move from individualism and personal feeling to self-transcendence and relationships with others. Understood biblically, praise is what draws us out of ourselves. It recognizes what we may not feel and sees what's easily missed: the forest, not just the trees; a bigger picture; what Paul Harvey called "the rest of the story."

The Bible is characterized by a story-telling "narrative sensibility." And so are we. All of us need a story to make any sense of life. We only see through the lens of some "storied" perspective. These stories may come from personal experience, family, job, or culture. They arise from domestic, commercial, political, or scientific perspectives, sometimes overlapping. We all experience life in terms of what James Baldwin called our "system of reality and what we assume ourselves to be."[2] Such systems account, in our view, for how the world works; they entail allegations of fact.

The Bible focuses on God, and the honor and praise God is due. This would be beyond reach but for the ways the stories of God resonate with experience, past and present. Marcus Borg speaks of the "macro-stories" of Scripture, identifying these as stories of liberation, homecoming, and acceptance.[3]

The challenge facing the church is to enable people to understand biblical narrative as the story of their own lives engaging other ways of understanding ourselves. How have we been "liberated"? How could we be? When have we experienced some return from what felt like exile? How has "homecoming," or a sense of that, been important for us? What does "acceptance" mean besides agreement and tolerance? The issue is not how we see ourselves in the Bible, but how the Bible slips into us: how the Bible "sees" us and creates the space for salvation, room for the rediscovery of passion that can breathe, an opening that can be filled by something we recognize as necessary and important.

This is not so much what we have to do as what we have to let the Bible itself do by getting out of its way. Not that interpretation is unnecessary: it's unavoidable. But in fairness to the text, interpretation should be governed by the logic of the text, not our own. Our own logic may be well motivated, as when we want to establish the Bible's relevance in terms most credible today. But then we're somewhat like the after-dinner host who, wanting to underscore the importance of the evening (or his or her own importance), spends more time introducing the speaker than the speaker does speaking!

The Bible is already familiar, if strangely so. As with Jesus' parables, it draws on known experience while ending with a twist—as when a wildly profligate son is welcomed home with a big party by his father, or a dishonest manager is praised for his shrewdness. The unexpected honor of God's generosity often comes as a surprise. So for us, too. In hindsight if not always at the time, we can see how surprising are the ways we are recognized and honored by love and blessing beyond anything we can take for granted or deserve. "Thank you, God" is offbeat. The closest we can come is, "Amazing! Praise God! Let's pass it on." The stones will cry out if we don't, as Jesus put it (Luke 19:40).

Looking at who we are in light of the grand stories of God and what God's love has made possible, our hearts fill with praise that includes but goes beyond gratitude. Praise, because this love is as awesome as it is mysterious, and unwarranted by

any logic of our own. The stories of God ignite generosity because that's what those stories are all about, and they are contagious. "Praise God, from whom all blessings flow" indeed!

However it sounds at first, this is no move from the outside
in. It's not laying the Bible on ourselves or others as have the
fundamentalists, this time calling it "story-telling." It is rather
trusting, or at least being open to, the evocative force of the text,
which works, through its differentness and strangeness, to
arouse recognition and response.[4] Then our own interpretation
takes into account the questions the Bible itself evokes rather
than simply reflecting our own.

What the Bible does is arouse and shape a response from inside out. What is persuasive is the resonance it sets up in the
specificity of experiences named and claimed by the text itself in
stories of liberation, homecoming, and acceptance; in stories like
those of the Exodus, the return from Babylon, and Nicodemus;
in stories like those of Jacob and Naaman; in the parables of
Jesus; in experience and conclusions like those of Paul—and in
our own lives where these stories find a counterpart.

Without this approach religious interest in "praise" or "giving as praise," as with so much else in the Bible, easily becomes
more rhetoric that no pulpit charisma or lectern eloquence can
make credible.

Praise breaks the crust of reluctant giving better than gratitude. In truth we are nowhere near as grateful as we should be.
We come to faith and church in varying moods and often with
misgivings. We can be glad and happy, but just as often we're
not. Sometimes we're not thankful, whatever our feelings
"should" be. Feelings cannot be jerked around just because
they're not appropriate.

Church giving often drops when people don't like the pastor, or the budget, or the church's commitment to a cause considered misguided. It's sometimes hurt by the church's denomination and its political stands on issues of justice. Generosity
can also be thwarted by trouble at home or in a close personal
relationship, by a problem at work or by financial anxiety, or by
generally feeling upset about everything.

Gratitude is unreliable. Understood as a subsidiary of praise it's more reliable, whatever the circumstances at hand. Praise ignites generosity because it focuses not on how grateful we are but on how great God is. "Sing to the LORD, bless his name; tell of his salvation from day to day. Declare his . . . marvelous works among all the peoples. . . . The LORD made the heavens. Honor and majesty are before him; strength and beauty are in his sanctuary. . . . Ascribe to the LORD the glory due his name; bring an offering, and come into his courts" (Psa. 96:2, 3b, 5b–6, 8). Not ascribe glory to the pastor, or the church or denomination. Don't bring an offering because of them. "Let no one boast about human leaders . . . Paul or Apollos or Cephas," as Paul said, citing prominent leaders of his day, including himself (1 Cor. 3:21–22). Did they make the heavens and the earth? Do they deserve praise? Is it into their "courts" or congregations that we "bring an offering"? Or do they point us to where praise belongs and what inspires the offering?

Involving what we prize and cherish, praise stimulates passion otherwise latent. Have you ever gone to a concert tired and worried about something? Then, as soon as the music began, you woke up and found yourself on the edge of your seat? That's an example of passion stirred up by something we like, prize, cherish—"praise." "He's the greatest violinist or she's the best jazz singer I've ever heard!" This is more than gratitude and if it's a mood of the moment it's different from how we had felt and it stays with us.

Usually excellence is involved—and it need not be on a concert stage. A truck driver was backing his eighteen-wheeler into an alley off a busy downtown intersection with barely an inch to spare on either side. He did it, and on the first try. Bystanders who had been watching applauded. Imagine what Jesus could do with this story. "There was a certain truck driver known to carouse with his buddies, and never more than before the day of a big haul. After a night at the tavern, he awoke in a daze, reminded by his friends that he was going to be driving to his destination in heavy traffic at the busiest time of day . . ." Then it might conclude with reference to all those righteous drivers, honking at the intersection, whose excellence on their own jobs was nothing next to the truck driver's!

Concerts, and truck drivers, can arouse praise—praise for excellence, praise for something outside ourselves that stirs us beyond what we had been feeling before. Giving praise, we give of ourselves more generously—as when the bystanders watching the truck driver, total strangers to each other, began looking at each other, shaking their heads, saying "What a guy!" several asking "Where do you work?" and even walking a block together.

Giving praise, we give ourselves more generously—as when after a good movie we find ourselves talking to people lined up to go in, unable to keep from commenting on the film; or as after that performance by the violinist, or the jazz singer, we talk to our seatmate instead of pretending he or she doesn't exist, perhaps at intermission with others as well who, given our usual ways, we would otherwise have passed by.

These simple examples suggest the big issue at stake with God and generosity. Praising God is like loving a great performance. Performance not just as an act, but as a full-throttled expression of something innate, inherent, and "organic" to the performer that awes and engages him or her, and us.

Look again at Paul's proclamation about God's performance to the Corinthians: "If God is for us, who is against us? . . . Who will separate us from the love of Christ? Will hardship, or distress, or persecution, or famine, or nakedness, or peril, or sword? . . . No . . . Neither death, nor life, nor things present, nor things to come, nor powers, nor height, nor depth, nor anything else in all creation, will be able to separate us from the love of God in Christ Jesus our Lord."

Hear Paul's voice. He can't possibly contain his excitement. He can't find enough words to describe what God does. The momentum of his rhetoric reaches a fever pitch. *God hits a grand slam!* While for us the game is not over, we know what's going to happen. The audience is going to be on its feet, and we're going to be jumping all over each other, unleashing more than a bottle of beer.

Paul's praise is aroused by God's magnificence. Lest all this sound light years away from anything we can recognize, we can recontextualize what we often face at church. "If God is for us, what's going against our church? Who will separate us from the love of Christ? Will low attendance on Sunday, a pastor we don't like, a budget that is controversial, poor giving, a feud on the church council, members who don't like us, hostility from neighbors who don't like our red and black banner outside that says "God Is Still Speaking," the anger of community leaders because they don't like our housing program and "those people" it draws into the neighborhood?

"No, in all these things we are more than conquerors, through God who loves us. For I am convinced that neither doubt nor fear, nor my ingratitude and foul moods, nor my spirituality or impatience with it, nor how much I like or dislike the pastor, nor my own highs or lows, nor anything else I can think of, will be able to separate me, and the rest of us, from the love of God in Christ Jesus our Lord."

Coming from praise, generosity is the ignition of this sense of victory won—or to be won, for we're always on the way. Remembering the twists and turns like those in Jesus' parables showing how good news can take us by surprise, we can move forward, and give, much more eagerly, right now.

Praise-giving is much like remembering the lyrics of a song we once liked. And, beyond gratitude, beyond "thank you," *we want to sing that song.* And if others can join us, all the better— which is one of the things that can happen at church, not just with singing and hymns, but with preaching, Bible stories, the conversation they arouse, and with giving.

This is the "gestalt" of generosity: the spirit, the driving force. Worship is its home. Praise is the essence of worship and the setting of giving. Worship is full of different personalities, moods, and personal circumstances. Literally, or figuratively, we come from north, south, east, and west. But we are one in the need to be reminded of something, or somebody, greater than ourselves. As Mahalia Jackson sang in another song:

Who made the mountain, who made the tree,
who made the river flowing to the sea,
and who hung the moon in the starry sky?
Somebody bigger than you and I.

In the concluding stanza, Jackson sings:

When I am weary, filled with despair,
who gives me courage to go on from there?
And who gives me faith that will never die?
Somebody bigger than you and I.[5]

Whatever one's taste in music, the spirit of this song, unleashed, is transformative. It loosens the grip of doubt or reserve that inhibits fuller participation in the church and releases generosity heretofore kept in check. This is what worship is all about. Under its influence, generosity thrives or falters.

A mission congregation was thriving. Worship was dynamic. The church had grown numerically. In its earliest days, it had grown spiritually and become a strong force in the lives of members. The best growth is by word of mouth. It's "viral": the result of catching a spreading bug! Such was the case with this congregation. Generosity and giving were never issues.

Then, for whatever reason, the pastor decided to invite in some American "fraternal workers," as they were called at the time. They were to develop a stewardship program for the congregation to strengthen giving and share different methods of doing so. The purpose was to shore up the foundation of the church financially so the leaders could plan the next steps with greater confidence.

Suddenly arguments erupted, not because the foreigners themselves were disliked, but because the congregation was divided about how now to proceed: should pledging be instituted, should the budget be planned in a congregational meeting or by a newly formed "stewardship committee," why should there be a financial secretary as well as a treasurer, should the budget be based on expected giving or on the church's ministry?

On and on it went, depressing the congregation, and leading to meetings after worship that had a chilling effect on Sundays. Members started staying away, giving was dropping, and the pastor started getting blamed for all this.

Finally, the fraternal workers left. The church became again what it had been—a vibrant congregation, giving not according to a program, but under the influence of the spirit for which the congregation had been known.

Good spirit alone doesn't raise money. Liking a concert doesn't often involve giving to the foundation that underwrites it, much less becoming a patron of the arts. Respecting a truck driver doesn't usually mean supporting the Teamsters' pension fund. Praising God doesn't guarantee generous giving. Programs and methods are often necessary to encourage giving to where it's most needed. These don't have to depress good spirit.

But for generosity to be aroused and programs to work, the church can learn a lot from evangelical congregations whose theology we may not be comfortable with, but whose fund-raising we often envy. As with the parable of the shrewd manager, why can't we be "shrewd" in our own ways of praising God? Need this be unnatural and contrived? Does this mean copying the contemporary worship styles of many evangelical churches, especially the larger ones, with the cross not too prominent so as not to turn off potential new members, no Bibles in the pews, and a big screen up front so nobody has to find a song in the hymnal?

Praise is *already* "shrewd" in the ways it reaches us. We just need to get out of the way. Who would have thought that against so many odds throughout history, Paul's words praising God's "grand slam" would prove true, even when only incompletely so with the game still on?

Praise is not always loud, or as declarative as Paul was. Sometimes it comes over us as a "still small voice" (1 Kings 11:12, KJV)—one we hear, one we ourselves utter in response. We can make a lot of noise, some of it reverent, much of it distracting. Preaching and music can be so "in your face" as to inspire a desire to get away from it all! The breathing space at the root of salvation means just that: room to think and wonder and pray; a chance not to have to listen to "still more"; a chance to be quiet before God, glad that something or somebody's there who actually is bigger than "you and I," and more noticeable than all the noise.

Generosity, like praise itself, isn't always experienced as a "grand slam," accompanied by a lot of fanfare and enthusiasm. It happens on its own. Good worship, including preaching and singing, help it to ignite. When it does, generosity is a flash of gratitude. Beyond that, it's also a quiet flame of awe—also reminding us to let that light, shining for us, shine for others as well.

USEFUL OR TRUE?

A forebear of the United Church of Christ in the nineteenth century, John Williamson Nevin was a leader of the German Reformed Church. Nevin was concerned about the revivalistic excesses of his day, spawned in large measure by another forebear, the president of Oberlin College, Charles Grandison Finney. A Congregationalist, Finney was well known for his "New Method" techniques of evoking an emotional response to the Gospel.[6]

Nevin was primarily concerned about the unity of the church, Finney about the conversion of the individual. Finney wore his faith on his sleeve, Nevin on his collar. For Nevin, praise is liturgical and centers on God's relationship with us through communion. For Finney, praise is personal and centers on our relationship with God. The formalities of worship are secondary.

The church these days is challenged to downplay the formalities, "get with it," and show more passion. It is true that we should be more personally direct in preaching and teaching the gospel. Often we're too cognitive, indirect, and nuanced, bending over so as not to sound like popular evangelicals. While he was an academic and president of a fine liberal arts college, Finney nonetheless inveighed against such head-centered reserve and emotional indirection.

Nevin was right in knowing that emotionalism can be subjectivism: passion can become a display of feeling, *my* feelings, at the expense of yours. The true passion of praise is the desire for something other than ourselves. However drawn I may be to the performance of the violinist or jazz singer—or truck driver—I am none of them. And whatever the workings of God's Spirit in my soul, drawing me closer to the divine, I don't become "God"! "One should use praise to recognize what one is not," wrote the Austrian novelist and philosopher Elias Canetti.[7]

Praise presumes a certain distance even while seeking to bridge that distance. Like love, it flames out when it becomes less a response to the other and instead an effusion of oneself. And so with generosity. Is this actually part of a *me* veneration, a useful form of "selfism," giving you something *I* think you should have regardless of what *you* want or need?[8] Or is it truly *God*-centered and so, in practice, something that keeps us from charging ahead—or simply failing to do much—without considering more carefully what's called for?

Nevin got to the heart of this issue. He said that too often religion is "a sublimated utilitarianism"—giving a nice calculation of profit and loss. "The notions of gain and godliness are apt to run wonderfully together in our minds."[9]

A church in the Midwest wanting to gain new members has a big sign outside saying, "You'll leave feeling better!" How useful! Which of us doesn't want to feel better? But many are the ways to feel better, especially on Sunday mornings. The church is not in the business of making people *feel* better but *be* better under the guidance of God. Praising God, I might feel worse because I come to realize I must do something I don't want to do—like get a divorce although I've wanted to avoid that, or declare bankruptcy instead of fooling myself any longer, or make amends to someone I've hurt, or think seriously about forgiving someone I can't.

Praise is not a free ticket to happiness. We praise the Artist. We praise the divine Michelangelo. God sees the *Pieta* in the stoniness of our recalcitrance and hopes we will too. But a stone is first a stone, and a lot of chipping away has to be done before we can see ourselves that way—and when we do it's likely to be "as through a glass darkly," only but dimly. The *Pieta* is "true" to the image in which we are created, and we might even glimpse it as it comes out. But is it useful? In and of itself, is any artistic accomplishment, however excellent, "useful"?

An economist said, "Faith will not be restored because people believe it to be useful. It will return only when they find that it is true." A political historian says that religion's "moral efficacy" is lost when it is simply linked to subjective assessments of interest. "Religion loses its own utility in proportion to which people become attached to it because of that utility."[10] We may be useful to one another, but if that's the primary reason we're drawn together, and invite others to join us, it won't be long before we lose our appeal. As circumstances and personalities change, utility proves to have a short shelf life.

Of course, generosity is useful. But is it true? As Carole King's popular song has it, "Is this a lasting treasure, or just a moment's pleasure? . . . Will you still love me tomorrow?" Which comes first if generosity is not only to ignite but last? Generosity, like love, is the *fruit*; praise, meaning prize or honor, the lasting *root*. Praise is our root response to God. It's the heart of worship. From it generosity grows. God is praise-worthy, our giving is praise-giving. This presumes that God is "truth-worthy," and so our giving, however useful, is foremost "truth-giving"—a way of telling the truth about God.

Stewardship is praise or *doxology* ("doxology" is from the Greek and Latin words for "praise"). Liturgically, as suggested earlier, we would do well to sing a version of the doxology before, not just after, the Sunday offering, and keep it up front in all financial appeals.[11] Rather than couching "praise" in the language of gratitude (that can follow), primary emphasis should be placed on the power of God—the overriding power from which no needs or feelings can separate us and which is at work in our midst, making hope real. (We may be guided by the selection from Romans 8 that opens part 3.)

In financial planning and appeals this means focusing on more than the church's program and how useful and promising it is. First it's "To *God* be the glory, great things he hath done," as the old gospel song puts it. Then we can express what, in response, we are doing. Let that glory not get lost in a budget—or confined to an opening or closing prayer, remaining another religious buzzword. Reclaim it by elaborating and celebrating what that glory means. *Spell out the praise that gives God the glory!*

Examples abound in the Bible where time and again hope and promise are inspired by what God did for Abraham, Isaac, and Jacob, then many others; hard times and endurance are recalled, victories cited. We can draw on more recent history and again today. *God's power has changed lives*, not only through big social and political movements of liberation, but also personally: addicts freed from a living hell; mental illness addressed; broken relationships dealt with, sometimes restored; healing beyond anything anticipated, physically or emotionally; deeper faith found amid spiritual estrangement. "In all these things we are more than conquerors through God who loved us. For I am convinced that neither death, nor life, nor angels, nor rulers, nor things present, nor things to come . . . will be able to separate us from the love of God in Christ Jesus our Lord!"

Spell out the praise that gives God the glory! No need to name names if that would be inappropriate. But specifying experiences like those just noted makes touchable and tangible what God's glory and our own praise are all about. Praise us—praise our church and its program? Of course, we have an important role in helping good things happen! But which of us who has gone through rough times can honestly say, "I did it." Glory be to my will power? Praise be to my strength?

Our own church and the caring of others make a big difference. But is that itself just their own doing, a matter of their own will power and strength? Anyway, how much of that could have been predicted, much less taken for granted and sustained—especially when the trouble at issue is awkward or controversial (as often happens, for example, with broken relationships, or problems with addiction)? What if giving, or receiving, forgiveness and acceptance are involved, beyond anything we alone could handle?

And what of the good times? The church is not a spiritual hospital or a therapy group. The help and healing it makes possible happen in the context of praise and worship. A large part of any recovery requires this anyway: who can get better in the depressing atmosphere of their own loneliness and distress? And lest the happy moments and good accomplishments play second fiddle to traumas, are these encouraged in the "prayers of the people" during worship? This can be hard when many prayers are requested for loved ones seriously ill, or for those who have lost jobs, or for overwhelming problems of suffering and injustice in the world.

But, "We must admit there will be music despite everything." To make suffering and injustice "the only measure of our attention is to praise the Devil."[12] Can we hear the music, share good news, maybe even show a sense of humor? We don't have a record of Jesus laughing, but how could he have kept a straight face when he saw people's reaction to his many ironic reversals that seemed to turn things upside down? A mustard seed moving mountains (Matt. 17:20)? Laborers who show up for work at the end of the afternoon getting paid as much as those who were there at the start of the day (Matt. 20:1–16)?

Praise God for irony and surprise! Praise God that life is not confined to our logic—and that what looks impossible or crazy often turns out to be good news, not bad. That, too, we can celebrate and share in prayer. This, too, ignites generosity!

Is all this just useful—or is it a matter of truth that means we'll still love each other tomorrow, when the excitement is over? What does one do with truth when at the time it doesn't seem to have any value? If I buy a good vacuum cleaner, that's immediately valuable and useful—or I return it and get another. This is what many do when they "shop" for a church. Is this one helpful? Does the other do a better job meeting my needs? Which offers the best deal in terms of demands on me? Which has services at the most convenient time? Which is most useful?

This is not necessarily wrong and it's inevitable. It also reflects and reinforces a mentality that should give us pause. Albert Borgmann, a philosopher of technology, speaks of the "device paradigm" whereby we draw back from "manifold engagement" with the things and people around us, and instead pursue products designed simply to deliver some circumscribed benefit. He contrasts what is involved in the central heating in our homes today with what heating a home entailed not that long ago, when the whole family had to be involved in cutting and stacking the wood, feeding the stoves and fireplace, and the like. Borgmann is not romanticizing the past. His is no "back to nature" call. But he is critiquing the present, challenging us to consider how we draw back from manifold engagement and construe what's valuable in terms of a narrower understanding of usefulness.[13]

But when what's valuable is limited by our own sense of what's useful, what do we do about ourselves much of the time! Concerned about our utility, many of us break our backs trying to be useful and worry that we're not being useful enough. No wonder we miss anything like a *Pieta* in ourselves, valuable in its own right, eager to come out, *worth just being*. We're always getting in the way of the Artist when we try to do all the work ourselves. We botch the job. Instead of any *Pieta*, what we get is a tired, unappealing version of the real thing. We're not good for "manifold engagement" with others because the "product" we're actually pursuing is our own utility, not the value of others and their own helpfulness.

My grandfather, prone to grave utterances as if delivering the Commandments, frequently admonished me as a youngster with an eleventh commandment: "Don't just sit there. *Do* something!" This was usually prompted by my greater attraction to the shade of the front porch on a hot summer day, an ideal place for reading rather than "doing something constructive" like mowing the lawn and besieging neighbors to let me mow theirs so that I could earn more "money for college" (and, no doubt, show what a hard-working, up-and-coming young man this grandson was).

A kindly soul as well as realistic, my grandfather had a point. But sometimes the word we really need to hear is, "Don't just do something. *Sit there!*" Blaise Pascal once said, "I have discovered that all human evil comes from this, one's being unable to sit still in a room." Pascal didn't say that sitting still is all we should do. He meant what Luther did when he said the fuller the day ahead, and the harder the work, the longer he had to pray. Scripture says we are to love God with all our heart, soul, and mind. "This is the greatest and first commandment" (Matt. 22:37). This is impossible without taking time to sit, be still "and know that I am God" (Psa. 46:10).

Unless we know the Society of Friends (Quakers) and have participated in silent meetings (worship), it's not natural to think of silence as an expression of giving or praise. We think of generosity as active. That activity is to be induced by words so generosity is sufficiently inspired and directed. The Quakers are known for outstanding giving—but they are a lot quieter! Among their numbers are some of the country's most highly regarded philanthropists. They have been in the middle of movements for peace and justice since their inception in the early days of the better known branches of Protestantism. Central to their faith is a commitment to silence as openness to the stirrings of God's Spirit.

Regarding giving, the Quakers trust this Spirit (the "Light of Christ within") to ignite generosity and the behavior this entails. There are no methods or techniques for doing so other than . . . silence. What is "given" first is silence. That is the implicit praise from which words follow, including concerns to support important work. The silence touches people in different ways—but it touches them as it engages them in all kinds of good deeds.

We are not Quakers. Our churches are more institutional. This is because of the way the Reformation began—not as a movement to replace Roman Catholicism, but to reform it. Our inheritance institutionally, sometimes liturgically, is actually

Roman Catholic. More importantly, our inheritance is biblical. While the first followers of Jesus shared everything in common (Acts 2:44), then, too, there soon arose the need for greater organization. But through it all, and in much subsequent Catholic, Orthodox, and Protestant Christianity, the Spirit—God's presence in the gathered community of believers, the church—is central, however differently understood.

"Institutional" became, and becomes, "unspiritual" when utility trumps truth. Then, wanting to stay useful and not become a nuisance, eager not to interfere with what is most expeditious culturally, politically or personally, the church and the gospel become tools of control. Its message is really, "Let us not disturb the peace—our own, the community's, the state's." So it is that the "institutional church" becomes suspicious of anything unpredictable that could lead to controversy—like God's Spirit, which, not by accident, was long buried in the Trinity behind "God the Father, God the Son." Heaven knows what God's Spirit might do, unleashed and given its coequality with formerly senior partners!

The issue is not the Quakers versus the rest of us, or "institutional" versus "spiritual." "In all these things we are more than conquerors" and ought to be fighting other battles—like making sure the truth of Paul's declaration can come across with as much clarity and excitement for us as it did for the apostle: "Nothing can separate us from the love of God." God is hitting a grand slam, the runners are coming home, the crowd is on its feet applauding and sharing the joy. This is victory none of us can win on our own. While the game is still on, we are given the outcome.

This truth is as much inward as outward. The Quaker's silence can become ours as we internalize these words and let them become our own. More quiet time in worship before or after prayers would be wise. Sometimes "silence" is helpfully guided by daily readings from a devotional or also from the Bible.[14] But time does need to be set aside for this. The last thing most of us can do is sit still!

It takes a while, sitting still, not to use that time to think of all the things we need to be doing. It's best to let these preoccupations run on their own until they subside. When this doesn't happen, it helps to remember that anything worthwhile takes practice. We can't play the piano overnight—or suddenly become physically fit.

We endure silence anyway, in the wake of death or when stunned by an upsetting diagnosis, or in the indifference or rejection of others.[15] We can co-opt those inevitable silences and make them part of a deliberate silence of our own—not becoming passive but more attentive to the God who is often found amid silence. The devil's not only in "the details" but often in the ways and words we find to fill an emptiness only God can fill.

The psalmist says, "Praise waiteth for thee, O God" (Psa. 65:1, KJV). This may be read "Praise is silent unto thee." One of the oldest Latin commentators reads it "Praise and silence belong unto thee."[16] The profound and the everyday are part of the same world. A dentist needs patients to sit still to do his or her job; so does a nurse giving an injection or an accountant distracted by a client's fidgeting as a tax return is prepared. So God seeks our silence, a space within our hearts where the divine Word may echo anew, "Behold, I make all things new!"

Of course, silence can be "useful"—to health, spirituality, and praise itself. Truth and usefulness belong together. It's a question of priority, as anyone understands who believes they're only loved because they're "useful" to the other. The natural response is to say or think, "You don't *really* love me." Being useful as a consequence of being loved is much different from being loved as a consequence of being useful.

And so with generosity. Plan, plot, and plead for it because it's a good thing to do, useful to the important work of the church, and it can't truly ignite—and last. People won't "still love you tomorrow" and you have to make a case for it all over again any time you need money, showing again how useful giving is. But let giving be praise, a matter of honoring and "prizing" and the heart of what worship evokes, and giving will become more natural—right, true, and good. That it's useful *follows*.

THE "ASK" OF PRAISE

Why would our wallets be more open than our hearts? Why would our "time and talent" be more freely shared than our good will? Paul was not always brimming with good will and a warm heart. He was often angry and upset by opposition he faced. He was not pleased by the behavior of some of the congregations he started or served. He did not praise God from a comfortable armchair with the world at his feet. He had to fulfill a difficult and dangerous mission to Jerusalem, thence to Rome and Spain. His life was continually at stake in the face of opposition from conservative religious authority and imperial power. But Paul was generous. And praising God, he asked a lot of those who would follow Christ.

Generosity doesn't always feel good. It can ask a lot of us. In the ancient world, generosity came to mean greatness of spirit. For early Christians, it came to mean greatness of Spirit—the holy Spirit, God's Spirit. In both usages, this s/Spirit was more than enthusiasm, although that can be one expression of it (enthusiasm comes from a word meaning "to be in God," the Greek *en-theo*).

Sometimes generosity is eager, willing, and enthusiastic; sometimes it's more a matter of duty or responsibility. In no case is it simply centered in personal emotion. It's a quality of temperament, a disposition, a bearing: what in Latin America is called a *manera de ser* ("manner of being"). This colors thought, feeling, and behavior, including giving. While consistent with the image in which we are created, generosity is not always evident unless drawn out by something outside ourselves. How often have we found that someone is actually thoughtful and interesting whom we had written off as aloof and uncaring? How often did that happen because we chose to talk with this person rather than remaining aloof and uncaring ourselves?

We should presume generosity because at heart that defines who we all are. Sometimes it won't show itself or may be withheld on purpose and find expression elsewhere. But stinginess and pettiness are "unnatural." Some may think that, theologically, this denies "original sin" and is too rosy a view of human nature. Even in that outlook "sin," original or otherwise, is not natural, otherwise it wouldn't be "sin," which means separation from our creator.

While we do live separated from God, and that's the human condition, for Christians Jesus is understood to have shared this condition completely, embodying and passing on God's Spirit to restore us to our original image as expressions of divine generosity.

We cannot pull off this restoration on our own. Otherwise we wouldn't need Jesus or the church. We need to be called out of the slumber of sin—the stinginess and pettiness that inhibit giving and narrow relationships with others. We need to wake up to how we really are and become ourselves.

Something inside us all awaits that call. And there's no better wake-up call than a strong "ask." *People like to be asked to give*, financially and otherwise. Too often we assume otherwise. We're shy. We don't want to be pushy or presumptuous. We know the limitations others face with myriad constraints on their time and financial resources. Perhaps we think others should know what they need to do without having to be asked. Also, asking makes us look needy. And when at first we don't get a response we're not about to ask again, because then any indifference or negative response will hurt twice as much. So it goes.

With that predisposition about asking, who would want to respond positively? It's as though we've got something up our sleeve, maybe something about which we're not sure ourselves. Why should I fund your uncertainty? Why should I support your ambiguity?

People do not like to be asked to give when there's nothing credible or compelling about our asking. We may think what we're asking for is important. But what of those receiving the request for help? As with money, so with other commitment.

One church needed new Sunday school teachers. The old ones had served for years and were getting tired of this responsibility. So the Christian education committee divided up phone calls asking for help from others in the congregation. The gist of the calls was, "We're wondering whether you would be willing to help out and teach Sunday school. Our current teachers have been doing this for years and are getting old. They're wonderful people but they can't do it anymore. Could you help? Maybe you could trade off with someone else and just do it for a few months."

Of course, the response was negligible. Of all those called, one offered to help "for the next month or so." In fact, this church did have good plans in the works. There was the prospect of a new curriculum and teacher-training assistance known to have been engaging and rewarding in several other churches. There were new families with children in the congregation. Maybe the Christian education committee itself was old and tired, or the plans were for next fall and help was needed right now. Whatever the reason, when we don't believe in ourselves, who else will? Too often we sell ourselves short in what could be inviting to others and arouse generous support.

And we sell others short. We all want recognition whether we admit it or not. An alumna of a wealthy university received a personalized fund-raising letter asking her to consider giving a substantial sum to the school. Ordinary approaches to donors are based on a breakdown of perceived ability to give, with solicitation and visitation determined accordingly. Her own job and earnings would not have put her high on such a list. She would never have been taken out to dinner by the financial development director.

Her response upon receiving the letter was to feel honored that anyone thought she could give that much. The university knew what it was doing. Their donor research was efficient enough to know which categories of alumni were likely to give the most, and no doubt some of that reasoning was followed.

But, as in this instance, whatever the category, the "ask" was an outright, unapologetic request for help. The university stated what it needed and addressed alumni with a clear challenge. That's showing respect! People are not "categories of givers."

This is a far cry from an approach like "we urge you to give what you can during these difficult times," coupled with a lack of direction about what the church actually wants and needs. No doubt the gift given to the university was not all the development office requested. But its appeal caught attention, made the prospective donor feel honored, and the ensuing response was greater than it would have been. People like to be asked to give, but not in a cloud of ambiguity when, moreover, they sense the presumption that they're unwilling or unable to give.

We must "make a case" for giving, which means making clear and compelling what the church needs and why. But the business we're in is God's business! The church is a franchise, authorized and branded by God. We operate under the guidance of God's Spirit made known in Jesus. Each of us is asked to consider again our own generosity, given God's own. The payoff is free but not cheap: life-changing satisfaction that takes doing. We're asked to make decisions we'd rather avoid, beginning with some that sound simple and yet often don't come about.

Could I be more generous, greater in spirit, more freely sharing of myself, by spending time with people I've avoided; by doing something I've been nervous about doing (like speaking up at a congregational meeting, or reading Scripture or just making an announcement during worship—when I've hated "public speaking"); by helping with a community project when I've always been uncomfortable around "do-gooders"; by taking on something the pastor has asked me to do that I'm not sure I want to do (chair the annual stewardship campaign, make visits to the homebound, lead a discussion)?

Could I be more generous at work? Can I care about others besides those I usually associate with, remembering that during times of uncertainty or due to the nature of the work they might appreciate someone else taking time to talk? Beyond being nicer, can I become less impatient with those I find irritating? A church sign said, "Remember! Everyone you meet today is fighting a battle for their life!" An exaggeration? For many, not by much.

Could I give more generously financially to the church? We're asked to take that to heart, too. But how can this or any other expression of generosity ignite, when it's allowed to remain latent, unexpressed as fully as it could be? Often it's driven to find expression elsewhere by our failure to ask for it up front and with conviction? As at the office, at home, or in other relationships, so with church: do we truly believe we're worthy of support?

The real question is whether we believe God is worthy of support. If God is worthy of praise, giving follows, financially and otherwise. But too often we let the "and otherwise" substitute for direct talk about dollars. While "time and talent" are important, solicitation of those forms of support during stewardship campaigns, however well-intended, can divert attention from the church's need for financial support, and our need to give it. People know money is needed, and talk of other ways to give can be, can at least seem like, beating around the bush. Some people are reassured by this, because they can't give the financial support they'd like to give. They should be reassured, but not when the need at hand is financial.

As a franchise of God's business, it's company policy the church is given to follow—not our own. We can't do the job according to "the devices and desires of our hearts."[17] We can't function according to our own planning and promotion. We can't choose our own "brand." We operate according to God's Spirit, expressed in praise like Paul's in Romans 8, in the psalms, and in all the great stories of Scripture.

Our planning, promotion, and "brand" show that this is a first-class steak house, not a burger joint. Our franchise follows rules that are not only "thou shalt not have a dirty kitchen," but "thou shalt welcome people gladly, make sure they're served promptly, and remember the quality with which you're associated." God's imperatives and "shall nots" are always associated with indicative "shalls": "Because I have delivered you from oppression, you shall . . ." "Because I care about the widow and orphan, you shall . . ." "Because I have healed you, you shall . . ."

Because I have given you the highest quality "product" imaginable, you shall remember who I am and what I do, be glad to be associated with me, and welcome and serve others.

Except for who God is and what God gives, this would be a tacky analogy, making the deity vain and self-serving. But God knows what happens when we forget whose quality business we're in and act as though we ourselves know best how to produce satisfaction and success.

Being honest and direct in asking for support and particularly for money, the biggest bogey, means asking for prayer, not just dollars. Some will tune this out or, emphasized too strongly, find it cloying, maybe embarrassing. Leave this to those spiritual people given to retreats and such. But again, we're in God's business, and prayer is a main feature. And it's one of the best ways to access God-given generosity.

This is not simply a way to raise money, a spiritual fund-raising technique. If it is, the offense is at once to others, whose credulity does not stretch that far, and to God, who is not credulous and sees exactly what's going on.

Sincerely encouraged prayer can make us look again at what we think we can do. A hospital chaplain asked a busy church leader to participate in an area coalition working on pressing housing issues. Knowing the leader had recently arrived on the job and faced many new responsibilities, rather than ask that he join the coalition and help raise financial support, the chaplain asked whether he would be willing to pray about helping out.

The leader had been all set to say no but could hardly say no, he wouldn't pray! So he did. Not down on his knees first thing in the morning, or late at night. But the chaplain's request preyed on him and, struck by her request, he took it to heart and thought about it at different times during the day.

A week or so later he realized that while he couldn't attend all the meetings of the coalition or raise money he should at least check further about what he might do. It turned out that at that time his representation of the denomination meant as much as financial support, and even if he could only attend every other meeting that would be helpful. So, having prayed about it, his instinctive "no" became an open-ended "yes." As it turned out, this grew into commitment greater than what the chaplain had thought possible.

Will we ask people to pray? Can we be so bold as to pray that they pray? Can we promote prayer, especially in relation to sensitive matters of budget planning and the solicitation of gifts? Can we ask people, beginning with the church's administrative bodies, to pray about what they give financially to the church?

The "ask" of praise is also a prayer. Pray the passage from Romans 8, again translating it into personal terms that speak to the moment. Help others do the same, perhaps with a sample prayer printed as an insert in the Sunday bulletin, or featured on the church's web site. Write your own.

We can't ask for support in the church without praising God, whose business we're in, and whose work changes lives and ignites responsiveness. God is glorified in prayer—and so is the budget, so are the givers. Often it's as though it's the other way around. We can so promote the budget and the reasons to support it that God is left implicit, maybe a forethought, perhaps an afterthought, not the heart of the matter. But then we're playing by our "rules" and not God's reality.

It's the "quality" and centrality of God that brand our own excellence. It's a focus on God's all-powerful love that inspires the greatest generosity and brings out a *manera de ser* like that of Jesus—a manner of being, not just a manner of giving suited to what we need this year. God is in the business of creating followers of Jesus and greatness of spirit, not just supporters of what the church needs this year.

The "ask" of praise draws attention to all that praise includes. Any congregation must take care of itself and serve its members wisely and well—on the analogy of a first-class steak house! But its clientele is worldwide. Fortunately, in addition to what can be done by the congregation for its own members and local community, denominations help extend the reach of praise. Church budgets include support for this broader reach of the church, sometimes called "our wider mission."

The congregation itself is part of the universal church of Jesus Christ, asked to embrace and advance his Spirit throughout the world. Each of us is incorporated into this universal body at baptism. The wider mission is accomplished not top-down, from us to the Third World (now called, more appropriately, the Two-thirds World or "developing countries") but in locally led partnerships and other on-the-scene alliances devoted to health care, education, economic development, disaster relief, human rights, as well as church-leadership training and church growth.

Too often we're vague in asking for prayer and support for this wider work of the church of which we, and our congregational budgets, are a part. We may promote special appeals for help during the year. But, overall, we're given to generalities. As with concerns at home, so abroad, prayers for "social justice" and "peace" can seem like more rhetoric, probably left-wing, at least not specific enough to compel attention in worship and even less in personal prayer. No wonder this "item" in the church's budget is often the most controversial, and something people are the least likely to support. Who wants to support something they don't understand, or that they have heard about ad infinitum and take as but another sign that the denomination is out of touch with how people in the pews feel?

Praise is universal because God is universal. Giving participates in a condition broader than anything we experience simply as individuals and personal believers. "If God is for the world, who is against it? Who will separate it from the love of Christ?" "For God so loved the world." Again we hear this echoed in "He's Got the Whole World in His Hands." Exclusivity here—thinking this good news is only for believers—has been doctrinally justified, but it's not Jesus justified. Considering the scope and spirit of his ministry, what's less than inclusive has no place in our faith and the work of the church.

Jesus has worldwide significance, even though the use of his name has been abused, and in that name much harm has been done. The Crusades were not just a phenomenon of years ago or an excess of other faiths. We ourselves practice as much again by damage caused by neglect of others beyond ourselves.

As praise directed to God, giving embraces others whoever and wherever they are, beginning in the local congregation. Our subjectivity and parochialism are transformed to include something broader than our own experience and needs. It becomes *inter*subjective and transparochial. Doxological giving is impelled by the excess of praise, not the logic of exchange—in the sense that God's love is "excessive," beyond anything we deserve or could ask for, not given in exchange for our merit and worthiness.

Such giving is driven, not by how much can I give, but by the question "What in the world will I do with all I have been given?" For the truth we have to deal with is not scarcity, but abundance; not neediness, but strength; not even injustice, but justice. What shall we do with all this abundance, all this strength and justice that God is, makes known, and works to bring about in the world? Once known, we can't stay away from it—anymore than we could breathe by somehow staying away from oxygen! God is life. As Jesus himself says, "I came that they may have life, and have it abundantly" (John 10:10b). And as Paul makes clear, nothing can separate us from that life and abundance. "Will hardship, or distress, or persecution, or famine, or peril, or sword? . . . No, in all these things we are more than conquerors through him who loved us."

We are asked to give witness to what God does, as we know this in Jesus, not try to do it ourselves. Justice and reconciliation are mine, says God, not yours. All you can do is act it out. Of course, "all" is a whole lot.

Will Campbell, a Southern Baptist preacher and civil rights activist, used to roam the backwoods of Mississippi visiting Ku Klux Klansmen on their front porches, always with a bottle of bourbon in hand. In the conviction that "Jesus died for the bigots as well," Campbell, well-known as a "n——- lover," never acted above it all, as though he wasn't in equal need of God's love and forgiveness. He got to know these people, and, at ease with his own conviction, spoke firmly without being defensive or argumentative. He praised God's love and, asking for bread, using the bourbon always at hand, invited the Klansmen to

share communion. Campbell testified to justice and reconciliation beyond anything he could accomplish.[18]

Asking the unjust to share with another of the unjust—himself—in praising God through the sharing of bread and bourbon! And so the abundance of God's love overflows in the giving of praise along with others, *whoever* they are.

Doxological giving is not governed by the logic of exchange
but the excess of abundance—abundance, as with Campbell,
that's no "pie in the sky" but practical and actionable right now.
There was no assured outcome of Campbell's work. Sometimes
those Klansmen were glad he left. Others were changed. But the
giving went on . . . and on. Just like God's. And so it is that justice and reconciliation happen—beyond what we alone can
make possible and amid much beyond our control.

Closer to home there are "Klansmen" we face, not only in
areas of injustice, but in domesticated versions of the same thing.
And sometimes they are us. Fearing the loss of power and influence over what we value and prize—not our own race, probably,
but our own jobs, pocketbooks, and our children's future—we
think in terms of what we lack, or could lose. We think of
"scarcity." God thinks of "abundance"; that's God's business. It's
our living untrue to that business that causes us big problems—
at home, in church, and everywhere else. Nothing's ever enough.

Praise asks us to look again at what we're given. How is this
abundance real for us and for others in a world more "needy"
than we are? In what ways is "neediness" really the issue? In the
perspective of abundance, scarcity and neediness are illusions,
easily inspiring feelings of personal inadequacy or, on the other
hand, patronizing benevolence. It's strength and justice God
gives us all to experience and share alongside one another.

As Campbell reminds us, this is God's doing supported by
us, not our doing supported by God. We think weakness needs
support. It's the other way around. Strength needs support. We
think injustice needs to be defeated. It's the other way around.
Justice needs to be celebrated. This isn't "just semantics." It's a
question of conviction and priority, and whether we're focused
on what pulls us up or, instead, on what drags us down.

If we respect the inherent strength and dignity of ourselves and others—including those who are seriously ill or otherwise oppressed, but also those who seem the most strong and successful—we don't let it languish and remain unengaged. If we respect the reality of God's justice, we testify to that, we tell stories about it, we find ways of acting on it, not with morose earnestness, but celebratively.

The real challenge is not how to overcome neediness, our own or anyone else's, but how to share generosity. After a sermon in a heavily guarded rally at a cathedral in Cape Town, Archbishop Desmond Tutu pointed a finger at the soldiers and riot police and said, "You may be powerful—very powerful. But you are not God. God cannot be mocked. You have already lost." But then, in a moment of unbearable tension, he came down from the pulpit, flashed that radiant Tutu smile, and began to bounce up and down with glee. "Therefore, since you have already lost, we are inviting you to join the winning side." The crowd roared, many of the police mixed in with the crowd or left, and the people began to dance.[19]

In thinking about major matters like what Will Campbell and Desmond Tutu faced, what we face can pale in comparison. We hear stories like those just told and still worry about the church budget, our own giving, and our children's future. We feel bound by limitation that is hard to overcome. The purpose of the church is to proclaim who God is and what God does right where we are. When Paul declared that nothing can separate us from the love that overcomes the odds, his "us" did not mean the early Christian martyrs, or people in the headlines of the day. He was not referring only to the big scale but the small scale too. After all, this is where we all live, including those on more obvious front lines of justice.

The church asks our support for the strength and abundance God makes ours, in ways little and big. In the help and hope we can offer one another. In learning what it means to live a life of faith amid doubt and discouragement. In recognizing us for the generous people we are and want to be. In helping us see and participate in God's work in the world, when it's easy to feel small and insignificant, driven to indifference.

We give, and ask for giving, to praise God, whose power and glory are the focus of worship, the church's program—and its budget. Praising God is contagious. It makes asking for support and giving it a lot easier, as natural as breathing and exhaling. That's life, which Jesus gives in all its abundance.

FACING OBSTACLES AND MOVING AHEAD

Ignite your congregation . . .

43 What's surprising about your church—and how is that surprise expressed? Sarah's laughter at God's surprise in Genesis 18 is part of what helped her and her husband, Abraham, to "keep on keeping on," as Gladys Knight sang. They continued faithfully against great odds into the future God promised. God is nothing if not exciting. How so your church, charged to convey God's message? Get in touch with God's surprise, perhaps with the help of Paul's declaration in Romans 8, and Jesus' parables. Let God's Spirit shape budget planning and financial promotion! People want to give to something not only worthwhile but exciting.

44 What's awesome about your church's worship? The choir? The minister? The overall spirit? What about the offering! Awe is part of praise and the atmosphere and motivation of giving. Consider ways in which the offering can be awesome, appropriately reflecting God's glory as much as anything else.

45 Are you a "fact fundamentalist"? What story, beyond the facts, does your checkbook tell? What story, beyond the facts of dollar amount, does your congregation's giving tell? What story, beyond the facts, does your own life tell? Consider how this narrative, "story" consciousness can shape our own and the church's self-understanding—and the ways we give.

46 A well-chosen contemporary reading accompanying one of the readings from Scripture can enhance, not diminish, the Bible and God's Word to us. This need not be "making the Bible relevant," but letting its own relevance resonate in a manner consistent with the liturgy and sermon. This is but the counterpart of music the choir sings that, without trivializing God (although that happens with much "praise music"), brings home what the praise of God is all about—as Mahalia Jackson did in her own way. This, too, is part of the Spirit that expresses, and ignites, good giving.

47 Consider asking people to come forward to place their offerings in a basket or plates on the altar, rather than give it passively in the pews. The same could happen with communion. This may be out of the question given the usual feelings about "coming forward" for anything during worship in many churches. But the question can provoke important discussion among church leaders. Praise is not passive. If not always demonstrative, "coming forward" is not catapulting down the aisle. It's a sign of respect for God— a willingness to stand up and be counted.

48 Make sure that "why we love the church," our church, comes through clearly in the sharing of prayer and announcements, printed and spoken, each Sunday. We give to what we love. Naming that love is part of worship and praise, and the invitation to give.

49 Develop a church photo exhibit and display it prominently. Feature personalities and the work of the church. No group shots. Encourage odd angles and special moments. The point is to help others see from a fresh perspective how God's praise works in the different ways people give of themselves. (This could also be done as a looping DVD/video recording.)

50 Have the Sunday school or youth group—maybe both, if those older are willing—develop a skit on key ministries the church budget makes possible. The theme if not the title is "I like giving to the church." Too often younger people are an appendage to giving, even if they're given offering envelopes. Help them understand and be recognized for their own importance!

51 Consider using, and building on, the "God Is Still Speaking" branding and emphasis of many United Church of Christ congregations to include "God Is Still Giving." Develop this good lead-in to financial appeals.

52 With the help of the worship committee, write a doxology, not as a replacement for what is usually sung after the offering, but before the offering, as part of the invitation. This could be two or three verses that praise God for the generosity already made known to us and shown in the work of the church.

AFTERWORD

A counselor speaks of different "languages" of love. For some, he says, love means quality time. For others, it's words of affirmation, gifts, acts of service, or physical touch.[1] A good relationship requires that we be multilingual—fluent in several languages. Knowing this, we nonetheless listen for our language when our partner is given to another. Words of encouragement may be discouraging to one who is looking for physical touch or practical assistance. Each language has its place, but not at the expense of the others.

We want our church to be open, affirming, and inclusive. It would help if that applied as well to the different "languages" we speak. It's easy to misunderstand one another if we listen for what we like at the expense of what's actually being said by someone else. One of us may be given to superlatives, praising God with unmistakable enthusiasm; others of us are more reserved, uncomfortable around such verbal excess. Some of us may be more concerned about outreach and service than Bible study or spirituality. We speak the language of faith in different tongues while wanting to say the same thing.

And so with generosity. Some of us are drawn to the reciprocity of giving. We look at it and speak of it in terms of what we have been given and how to use that most faithfully and effectively. Others of us are drawn by the prospect of new things to come. We see giving as enabling greater openness to what is already before us or what lies ahead. Others of us think of giving as part of what it means to worship God.

All of us are generous in different ways. All of us need to be engaged in different ways. As with the languages of love, so with the languages of generosity. No one tongue can say it all. This gets forgotten in much church budget planning and financial promotion. Faith-based giving competes with an emphasis on supporting the budget. What's "spiritual" is easily pitted against what's "good business." This is as false as emphasizing one way of expressing love at the expense of others.

The key to igniting generosity is engaging the different ways it is experienced and expressed. This may also be the key to a better understanding of ourselves. We are generous people, often stifled by problems and pressures that speak more loudly than anything else. But God's voice is there, amid the earthquake, wind, and fire. And that still small voice speaks in all kinds of ways. And one of the things it says is "I will be with you always." Hearing this, we can live and love, and give, more freely than ever before.

NOTES

INTRODUCTION

1. Marc D. Hauser, *Moral Minds: How Nature Designed Our Universal Sense* (New York: HarperCollins, 2006); Steven Pinker, *The Blank Slate: The Modern Denial of Human Nature* (New York: Penguin, 2003).

2. Quoted by Alan Schom, *Emile Zola: A Biography* (New York: Henry Holt, 1988), 25.

3. John L. McKenzie, *Dictionary of the Bible* (New York: Macmillan, 1965), 760. This *YS* root accounts for the Hebrew name *Yeshua* (Jesus), common in New Testament times, literally meaning "God is saving us."

4. Jim Wallis, *Faith Works: Lessons on Spirituality and Social Action* (London: SPCK Publishing, 2002), 14.

PART ONE: Giving and Receiving: Reciprocal Generosity

1. From *Who's on First* (Amazon Digital Services, 1997), also Lawrence Kushner, *God Was in This Place & I, i Did Not Know: Finding Self, Spirituality, and Ultimate Meaning* (Woodstock, VT: Jewish Lights Publishing, 1991), 13–14.

2. Ibid., 47–48.

3. See Genesis 32:27–28, 35:10.

4. Simone Weil, *Gravity and Grace* (New York: G.P. Putnam's Sons, 1952), 10.

5. Psalm 66:13b–14; compare also Psalm 22:25b, 61:5, 116:14, 18. See *The Torah: A Modern Commentary* (New York: Union of American Hebrew Congregations, 1981), 196, n.2.

6. See, for example, Exodus 20:1–2, Malachi 6:10.

7. For another version of this point, see William C. Green, "Honest to God," (Cleveland: Stillspeaking Daily Devotional, United Church of Christ Writers' Group, Local Church Ministries), March 27, 2009.

8. For a better understanding of "testimony," see Lillian Daniel, *Tell It Like It Is: Reclaiming the Practice of Testimony* (Herndon, VA: Alban Institute, 2005).

9. See *Inspiring Generosity* (Cleveland: Stewardship and Church Finances Ministry, Local Church Ministries, United Church of Christ, 2004), 48–49.

10. Daniel, *Tell It Like It Is.*

11. See Barbara J. Essex, *Bible for Vital Congregations* (Cleveland: Pilgrim Press, 2008).

PART TWO: Giving and Difference: Open Generosity

1. See Frederick Buechner's reflection in *Wishful Thinking: A Theological ABC* (New York: Harper & Row, 1973), 69.

2. Personal experience.

3. Meeting of the United Church of Christ Stillspeaking Writers' Group, Cleveland, March 23, 2009.

4. See Randy Hammer, *52 Ways to Ignite Your Congregation: Practical Hospitality* (Cleveland: Pilgrim Press, 2009).

5. See "Are You Ready to Talk about Your Church?" and "16 Ways to Say, 'I Love My Church'" (Cleveland: The Stillspeaking Initiative, United Church of Christ, 2008).

6. "He's Got the Whole World in His Hands," traditional African American spiritual.

7. C. S. Lewis, *Mere Christianity* (New York: Macmillan, 1943), 174–75.

8. Annie Dillard, *Teaching a Stone to Talk* (New York: Harper Perennial, 1988), 40.

9. For a thorough development of this perspective, see Ronald A. Heifetz, *Leadership without Easy Answers* (Cambridge and London: Harvard University Press, 1994).

10. Chris Prentiss, *The Alcoholism and Addiction Cure: A Holistic Approach to Total Recovery* (Los Angeles: Power Press, 2007), 164–65.

11. Ian H. Birnie, *Trevor Huddleston: People with a Purpose* (London: SCM Press, 1973), 43.

12. Cleveland: United Church of Christ Writers' Group. For further information about resources this group may be contacted at www.ucc.org/writers-group.

13. The use of "business people" may include attorneys and other professionals. The point is to emphasize the "money-making" ministry of those not ordinarily associated with the delivery of services in the manner of doctors, nurses, teachers, and the like, which can more easily be construed in terms of church values.

PART THREE: Giving as Praise: Doxological Generosity

1. Claus Westermann, *Praise and Lament in the Psalms* (Atlanta: John Knox Press, 1981), 5–35, 152–62.

2. From James Baldwin, "Letter from a Region in My Mind," in *The New Yorker* (November 17, 1962), 86.

3. Marcus Borg, *Meeting Jesus Again for the First Time* (San Francisco: HarperSanFrancisco, 1994), 119–40, especially 133.

4. David Tracy, *The Analogical Imagination* (New York: Crossroad, 1981), 115ff.; Walter Brueggemann, *Theology of the Old Testament* (Minneapolis: Fortress Press, 1997), 1–114.

5. Hy Heath, Sonny Burke, and John Lang, "Somebody Bigger Than You and I," © 1951 Bulls-Eye Music, Inc.

6. Richard E. Wentz, *John Williamson Nevin: American Theologian* (New York: Oxford University Press, 1997); Keith J. Hardman, *Charles Grandison Finney 1792–1875: Revivalist and Reformer* (Grand Rapids: Baker Publishing, 1990).

7. Elias Canetti, *The Secret Heart of the Clock: Notes, Aphorisms, Fragments 1973–1985* (New York: Farrar, Straus and Giroux, Noonday Press, 1991), 73.

8. Luc Sante, "Be Different! (Like Everyone Else)," *The New York Times Magazine* (October 17, 1999), 142–45.

9. From "Judgment and Duty," *German Reformed Messenger* 26:20 (January, 1861), cited by Wentz, *John Williamson Nevin*, 56.

10. Barbara Ward, *Faith and Freedom* (New York: W.W. Norton, 1954), 265; Pierre Manent, quoted by Sanford Kessler, *Tocqueville's Civil Religion: American Christianity and the Prospects for Freedom* (Albany: State University of New York Press, 1994), 182.

11. See part 1, "Facing Obstacles and Moving Ahead," #15, p. 43.

12. Jack Gilbert, *Refusing Heaven* (New York: Alfred A. Knopf, 2005), 3.

13. Albert Borgmann, *Technology and the Character of Contemporary Life* (Chicago: University of Chicago Press, 1984), 41–42.

14. One such devotional has been written by William C. Green, *The Big Secret of Giving: Hidden Treasurers in Life and Church* (Cleveland: Congregational Vitality Initiative, Local Church Ministries, United Church of Christ, 2007).

15. See "Enduring Silence," a devotional by Christina Villa in *The Best of the Stillspeaking Daily Devotionals* (Cleveland: United Church of Christ Writers' Group, 2009), 18.

16. Noted by C. H. Spurgeon in "Praises and Vows Accepted in Zion," *Spurgeon's Sermons*, vol. 3 (Grand Rapids: Baker Books, 2003), 124.

17. "We have followed too much the devices and desires of ours hearts," appears in many prayers of confession, originally Anglican.

18. See conversation with author, Frye Gaillard, *Race, Rock, and Religion: Profiles from a Southern Journalist* (Charlotte, NC: East Woods Press, 1982), 29f.; also *Will Campbell: A Radical Prophet* (Macon, GA: Mercer University Press, 1997); *Will Campbell, Forty Acres and a Goat: A Memoir* (Atlanta: Peachtree Publishers, 1986).

19. Jim Wallis, *Faith Works: Lessons on Spirituality and Social Action* (London: SPCK Publishing, 2002), xxix–xxx, 276.

AFTERWORD

1. Gary D. Chapman, *The Five Love Languages* (Chicago: Northfield Publishing, 2004).

BIBLIOGRAPHY

Christopher, J. Clif. *Not Your Parents' Offering Plate: A New Vision for Financial Stewardship*. Nashville: Abingdon Press, 2008.

Coles, Romand. *Rethinking Generosity: Critical Theory and the Politics of Caritas*. Ithaca and London: Cornell University Press, 1997.

Copenhaver, Martin B. *To Begin at the Beginning: An Introduction to the Christian Faith*. (Revised and expanded), 63–142. Cleveland: Pilgrim Press, 2002.

Daniel, Lillian. *Tell It Like It Is: Reclaiming the Practice of Testimony*. Herndon, VA: Alban Institute, 2005.

————. "Are You Ready to Talk about Your Church?" Cleveland: The Stillspeaking Initiative, United Church of Christ, 2008.

Daniel, Lillian, and Martin Copenhaver. "Are You Ready to Talk About Money In Your Church?" Cleveland: The Stillspeaking Initiative, United Church of Christ, 2008.

————. "16 Ways to Say, 'I Love My Church.'" Cleveland: The Stillspeaking Initiative, United Church of Christ, 2008.

Dick, Dan R. *Revolutionizing Christian Stewardship for the 21st Century: Lessons from Copernicus*. Nashville: Discipleship Resources, 1997.

Durall, Michael. *Creating Congregations of Generous People*. Herndon, VA: Alban Institute, 1999.

————. *Beyond the Collection Plate: Overcoming Obstacles to Faithful Giving*. Nashville: Abingdon Press, 2003.

Essex, Barbara J. *Bible for Vital Congregations*. Cleveland: Pilgrim Press, 2008.

Green, William C., Mark Suriano, and Christina Villa. *Inspiring Generosity*. Cleveland: Stewardship and Church Finances Ministry, Local Church Ministries, United Church of Christ, 2004.

Green, William C. *The Big Secret of Giving: Hidden Treasures in Life and Church: A Stewardship Devotional*. Cleveland: Congregational Vitality Initiative, Local Church Ministries, United Church of Christ, 2007.

Heifetz, Ronald A. *Leadership without Easy Answers*. Cambridge and London: Harvard University Press, 1994.

Hoge, Dean, Patrick McNamara, and Charles Zech. *Plain Talk about Churches and Money*. Herndon, VA: Alban Institute, 1997.

Hudnut-Beumler, James. *Generous Saints: Congregations Rethinking Ethics and Money*. Herndon, VA: Alban Institute, 1999.

Powell, Doris R. *Stewards in the Household of God: A Resource for Holistic Year-Round Stewardship*. Cleveland: Stewardship and Church Finances Ministry, Local Church Ministries, United Church of Christ, 2008.

Powell, Mark Allen. *Giving to God: The Bible's Good News about Living a Generous Life*. Grand Rapids: William B. Eerdmans, 2006.

Reeves, Michael, and Jennifer Tyler. *Faith and Money: Understanding Annual Giving in Church*. Nashville: Discipleship Resources, 2003.

Robinson, Anthony B. *Transforming Congregational Culture*. Grand Rapids: William B. Eerdmans, 2003.

——— . *Leadership for Vital Congregations*. Cleveland: Pilgrim Press, 2006.

Schwarzentraub, Betsy. *Afire With God: Becoming Spirited Stewards*. Nashville: Discipleship Resources, 2000.

Smith, Christian. *Passing the Plate: Why American Christians Don't Give Away More Money*. New York: Oxford University Press, 2008.

Stackhouse, Rochelle. *The Gifting God: Change the Way You Look at Giving*. Cleveland: Stewardship and Church Finances Ministry, Local Church Ministries, United Church of Christ, 2007.

Wright, Lauren Tyler. *Giving—the Sacred Art: Creating a Lifestyle of Generosity*. Woodstock, VT: Skylight Paths Publishing, 2008.

Wuthnow, Robert. *The Crisis in the Churches: Spiritual Malaise, Fiscal Woe*. New York: Oxford University Press, 1997.